ek dra hierdie boek
op aan Dwane en Anton
wat ek gesien het in
die hemel. Weet asb
my maats ek sal julle
weer sien in die hemel.
wens ek was by julle.
het werklik hart gewerk
om die boek te skryf voor
Jesus ons kom haal. God se
hy sal Jesus you stuur.

I dedicate this book to Dwane and Anton,
the boys I met in heaven.
You are my friends and I will see you again in heaven.
I wish I was with you.
I worked hard to write this book
before Jesus comes to fetch us.
God says He will be sending Jesus soon.

Thank you

TO MY ABBA FATHER, JESUS, AND MY BEST FRIEND, HOLY SPIRIT – Thank You for making me taste and see that You are the God of the supernatural. Thank You that You have never, nor will You ever, leave me or forsake me. Your love is all I need. May this book bring glory to Your Holy name. Thank You for Your breath in the book, Lord – Your precious *Ruach HaKodesh*.

TO MY FAMILY – Thank you that you are walking with me in the Spirit, living with me in the supernatural, and that you are always ready to cover me with your love. Thank you for the freedom all three of you give me to go and preach the Gospel of Jesus Christ around the world.

TO MY PERSONNEL AT THE MINISTRY that have the same fire and love to serve Jesus Christ as I do – I see all your long hours and hard work. Thank you for your beautiful hearts and your passion for this ministry and spreading the Gospel.

TO MY PARTNERS AND FRIENDS OF THE MINISTRY – Thank you for your support and your continual prayers of faith that lift my hands. You have become my friends. For the people all over the world that pray for us and send us e-mails and letters, thank you all! These letters are a constant stream of joy and make me want to fight the good fight with more strength, courage, and valour.

TO EVERYONE WHO CONTRIBUTED TO THIS BOOK – Judike, I will never be able to thank you enough for helping me. You are a real go-getter. When I look at you, I see Jesus in your eyes. Holly, you were handpicked to let your expertise flow through this book for the building of His Kingdom. Your eagerness to serve is precious in the sight of the King. Jules, you were sent by God for a time such as this. Cilmi, your beautiful touch flowing from your beautiful heart makes this book one of a kind. Destiny Image – thank you for sharing our vision!

Destiny Image® Publishers, Inc.
PO Box 310, Shippensburg, PA 17257-0310
"Promoting Inspired Lives."

ISBN 10: 0-7684-4208-7
ISBN 13: 978-0-7684-4208-3

For Worldwide Distribution
Printed in the U.S.A.

This book and all other Destiny Image, Revival Press, MercyPlace, Fresh Bread, Destiny Image Fiction, and Treasure House books are available at Christian bookstores and distributors worldwide.

For a U.S. bookstore nearest you, call 1-800-722-6774.
Or reach us on the Internet: www.destinyimage.com.

1 2 3 4 5 6 7 / 16 15 14 13

A young boy's experience of
Heaven and Hell

Heaven

&

Hell

from **GOD** *a message of faith*

Preface

Part 1: The story continues...

Part 2: Walking in the Spirit

Epilogue: Where Aldo is today

Preface

I knew I would need faith for this road of recovery with Aldo, but I wasn't sure how faith actually worked. *My* faith was not enough, and I soon realized I needed the God kind of faith. One can only receive this kind of faith when you live, walk, and breathe in His Kingdom; serving the King of kings with your whole heart. The Word of God says: *'The just shall live by faith'* (Hebrews 10:38). I have found the more intimate my relationship with Jesus becomes, the easier it is to believe. The walk of faith is something many try to teach, but few actually live. To live by faith costs a price. Nothing more, and nothing less, than your life – this is to be completely surrendered to Him.

To me, faith is simply: *confidence in God.*

To know, that I know, that I know, that God is who He says He is. When He says He will do something, then He will. Even if it doesn't look like it is going to happen right away, it will come to pass in His perfect timing, because He sees and orchestrates the big picture. All we need to do is to remain confident in Him.

I have also learned to recognize the lies of the enemy, and how to fight against doubt and fear.

People ask me, 'How can you still believe after five years, Retha? Don't you think it is time to give up, and move on with your life?'

Well, the answer to that is easy – my faith is in the God who is who He says He is, and not in my own abilities.

My house is now built on the Rock, which is Jesus Christ. I used to build my house on sinking sand, with fear as the building blocks, and my own strength as the cornerstone. When the storm hit, and tragedy turned my life upside down, God's promises laid a new foundation on the Rock, and by His grace I now build my house with faith, hope, and love. In

Jesus, I can remain standing on the inside, because I know the circumstances raging on the outside can't move me.

This is a lonely road, and I have learned that my faith must conquer the difficult situations I face. I cannot dare listen to words of unbelief from those people who doubt that God is a God of the impossible. Words of unbelief will only tear down what I am working so hard at building up.

The life Aldo lives is one of Kingdom reality; walking by faith and not by sight. Faith is the link to the supernatural, and faith speaks the plan God has for us in the natural world, into fulfillment. When you look at this young boy's body and his outside condition, you can easily be deceived by what you see. The deceiver will always try and lure people to the flesh, distracting them from faith in the promises of God.

In this book, you will learn more about the supernatural road we are walking on with God in His Kingdom of light. Aldo is God's ambassador. He receives revelation knowledge from the Holy Spirit and his letters contained in this book share these insights with the rest of the world. He lives in God's power, and through his life, I have learned that God only needs a willing vessel, not necessarily a perfect one.

To live in His Kingdom, we are required to allow God to work through us. This is only possible when we die to self and to our own agendas, and live only to please Him. In Aldo, I can see the difference between *trying to die* and being *truly dead* to the world, because nothing of the flesh impresses him anymore.

The day will come — and I hold on to that hope — that we will reap the good harvest from the seeds of faith that we are sowing now. Faith is a gift from God, a spiritual reality only God can provide.

In this supernatural journey, *I know, that I know, that I know* – **Jesus is truly alive!**

Jesus sê sy gees sal in die boek wees. Die boek moet wereld wyd gaan.

Jesus says His Spirit will be in the book.
The book must go over the world.

PART 1:

The story continues...

Introduction: The journey continues

Jesus will help you with everything in your life. God will send His son to take us to Him. I saw Him on His throne We will all tell Him what we did for Him on earth. Jesus wants your life. He loves you so much. Please believe me. God gives everyone the same chance to accept Jesus as saviour Will you believe me? There is a heaven and a hell. We will worship Him the whole time in heaven.

This is where we ended off in our book *A Message From God*.

This chapter is only a short summary of our first book and it paints the background so that you can share with us the miraculous testimony of a young boy's supernatural experience of heaven and hell, from then till now.

At the outset of 2004, to an outsider looking in, my life could have been described as perfect. I was crowned as Mrs. South Africa, and my business was flourishing. I had a wonderful husband at my side, two beautiful boys to fill the quiver...and I was totally sold out to the world and all the glitz and glamour it had to offer me.

For the most part, my life revolved around my children. After struggling to conceive with both of them, I was like a protective hen over her chicks. My kids were not allowed to drive with anyone besides me. I was determined to protect them – *I* will take care of them, *I* will provide, *I* will protect, *I* will decide. *I* was controlling everyone around me. My entire world revolved around me, myself, and *I*, until the Lord brought me to face a big red stop sign in June 2004. There I learned how weak *I* really was.

An automobile accident changed the course of my picture perfect life, irrevocably. My husband, Tinus, our two sons, and I were returning home from one of my speaking engagements as Mrs.South Africa. We were on a busy highway, when a stationary vehicle in the middle of the road, left Tinus no other option but to swerve off the road to avoid a collision and to miss the oncoming traffic. Josh, my youngest child, was two years old at the time, and Aldo, my eldest, was twelve. Both the children were thrown from the vehicle on impact. We found Josh lying near the wreckage, but Aldo was nowhere to be found.

After what felt like an eternity, I found Aldo's limp body on the other side of the highway. His skull was cracked and hot blood was trickling from his ears. He was already in a coma. I heard the sound of another oncoming vehicle that swerved off the road to avoid the accident scene, and I immediately jumped up from where we laid hidden. At that moment, the vehicle's headlights completely blinded me, and suddenly my whole body started shaking. When my body relaxed, I felt a fire running over me, followed by the peace of God that truly transcends all human understanding. Although I kneeled at my child's broken body, I still experienced a peace that was totally supernatural.

Nothing can prepare any parent for such a moment. Since then, His peace has never left me. Yes, I do go through valleys and over hills just like the rest of you, but His peace has always been with me. There, at the side of the road, kneeling beside my unconscious son, I met the God of the supernatural.

Aldo was immediately airlifted to the hospital. The emergency medical team tried to reassure us that he was in good and capable hands, but they also warned us that he was badly hurt, and they couldn't guarantee that he would pull through. Their biggest concern was his head injury that resulted from the intensity of the impact. We later found out that his midbrain, brainstem, and the front part of his left lobe sustained the most damage. For weeks after the accident, Aldo was still in a coma.

One night I had a dream, and in this dream I could clearly see that my son was at the brink of death. In fact, I thought it would be mere moments before he breathed his last breath. In the dream, I saw his fingers shrinking and his lips turning blue. (In the natural, we had been vigorously fighting for his life for weeks, but he showed no signs of improvement and he was still in a coma. To tell you the truth, I was starting to doubt if we could win this battle.)

In the dream I said to him, 'Aldo, Mommy is going to let you go to Jesus now.'

But he looked at me and replied back, 'No, Mom. You must speak life over me!'

I didn't really know what he wanted me to say by 'speaking life,' but the Holy Spirit, our Wisdom from God, came to my aid. Suddenly, the words of John 10:10 were illuminated in my heart. It was as if a light was switched on, and I knew and understood that the devil came to kill, steal, and destroy – but Jesus Christ came that we may have life and life in abundance! This was the life Aldo wanted me to speak over him!

> 'The thief does not come except to steal,
> and to kill, and to destroy.
> I have come that they may have life,
> and that they may have it more abundantly.'
> *- John 10:10 -*

In the dream, I immediately started speaking life over Aldo as he had told me to do. I could visibly see the strength and life slowly returning to Aldo's crumpled body. His fingers started growing and color returned to his lips.

I woke up very puzzled by the dream, but I knew something had changed and that we were at a turning point in his recovery.

One week passed, seemingly with no change in his condition. He was still in a coma, and the doctors still had little hope for his recovery. After my dream, I had hoped to see an immediate change in his condition, but nothing happened. His frail little body still seemed lifeless. Nevertheless, Tinus and I took turns, and we kept on speaking Scriptures, proclaiming the life Jesus came to give, over and over into Aldo's spirit. The dream was so real to me; I knew God gave it to me for a very specific reason.

What I did not comprehend at that stage, was the spiritual law of sowing and reaping. First, there needs to be seeds of life in the ground before a harvest of life can spring forth. By speaking words of life you sow life, and with time you will see the fruit of life come into your storehouse.

Aldo's heart rate was still very low, and his chance of survival was, medically speaking, hanging by a thread. I closed my ears to the doctor's reports and repeatedly said, 'Aldo, you shall have life in abundance!'

I remember standing at the end of his bed, listening to the machines, and feeling totally helpless. I realized that I had no control over what would happen next; whether he lived or whether he died, was not in my hands. It doesn't matter who you are, or how much money and influence you have; God, and God alone, holds the power over life and death. This mother that was always in full control of each and every situation, suddenly realized she could do nothing!

In my desperation, I ran to the room next to ICU where we were sleeping, pulled my jacket over my head, and called out to God with everything inside of me. I called with my entire being – spirit to Spirit...and God answered. The Word of God tells us; *those who seek God, will find Him*! At that moment, He shined a bright light into my heart, and my whole life seemed to flash before my eyes. It is a very sobering experience when you look at your life through God's light (His light is so bright, it exposes everything), and then realize that nothing is hidden from before His eyes.

It was here that I came to the end of myself, and all I could utter was, *'Father, help me! I am lost!'* The, *I* in my life was always written in a capital letter, but in the presence of the Almighty I AM, the *I* had no other choice but to bend its knee. In His presence, pride cannot stand. There every knee bows spontaneously and every tongue proclaims that Jesus is Lord (see Philippians 2:10-11).

Only once you are faced with the reality of who God *really* is do you begin to understand for what purpose He has created you – to be one with Him, totally dependent on Him, loving Him from a pure heart, and worshipfully fearing Him. I know today that total dependency on God is the door to intimacy with Him. Intimacy was something I never understood before; in fact, I didn't even know it existed! For forty years of my life, I worshiped God from my *flesh*. God is spirit, and that is why He says He is looking for a people who will worship Him in *spirit* and *truth*. That is the reason why I could never hear His voice.

> 'But the hour is coming, and now is,
> when the true worshipers will worship the Father
> in spirit and truth;
> for the Father is seeking such to worship Him.'
> *- John 4:23 -*

But on this day, things were different. My spirit connected to God's Spirit, and I heard God speaking to me in an audible voice: *'Retha, do you believe My Son Jesus paid the full price on the cross; that His sacrifice was perfect and complete?'*

I was raised in the Church and knew the answer to that question from my dogma. I immediately answered, 'Yes, Lord.'

Although I was a churchgoer, I didn't really know God, or fully understand the blood of Jesus. I found out that day, that there is a big difference between *knowing about* Jesus and actually *knowing* Him. To know Him is truth and life. To know about Him is rules, regulations, and tradition. Please, I urge you to listen carefully to my words today – to belong to a church is not enough! The King is seeking a love relationship with His Bride and a love relationship is much more than an hour on a Sunday.

After Father God asked me that initial question, He spoke to me in the most loving voice I have ever heard: *'Retha, My Son gave His life for you. Now I am asking you – are you willing to give your life to Me?'*

At that moment, God showed me the cross and Jesus hanging on it. And here, for the first time in my life, I understood the blood of Christ. It is the blood of the Lamb that truly and completely frees us, heals us, and restores us.

I then saw a veil drop from heaven and as it tore open; I saw the outer court, the inner court, and the Holy of Holies. I also intrinsically knew the life I had led for the past forty years was only built in the outer court.

God said to me, *'I want you to take off all your masks and come follow Me. I am not interested in your pretenses or superficial good works, but in your entire life! You must repent of your sin and turn your back on it. I want to cleanse you with the blood of Jesus. Only the blood of Jesus can cleanse sin and remove it from you as far as the East is from the West. I will never think upon it again once the blood of the Lamb has washed it clean.'*

Down on my knees, face to the ground, I repented as events flashed before my eyes and as the Holy Spirit convicted me in my heart. Finally, after forty years, I was freed in one moment. I could see the selfish *I* on the cross with Jesus, because I had died and my life was now hidden with Christ in God (see Colossians 3:3). But I was also raised with Him to a new life! Like Paul, I could now also say it is no longer I that live, but Christ that lives in me; Jesus, my hope of glory! (see Galatians 2:20; Colossians 1:27.)

Thereafter, God said to me, *'You need to be filled with*

My Holy Spirit.'

'Father, You know how many times I have asked this of you before. Why can I only receive this gift now?'

Knowingly, His reply came, *'I could not fill you My child, because there was no place for the Holy Spirit in your life. You were too full of yourself. A person needs to come to Me empty (dead to self), before I can fill him with My Holy Spirit.'*

I always thought of myself as building my house on the Rock, only to discover with a shock, that my life was built on sinking sand. What I had been seeking for so long, through striving and my works, God gave me in an instant. He could fill me with His precious Holy Spirit because I was finally empty of 'Retha.' I handed my life over to God and gave the Holy Spirit full permission to take over, and then God said, *'Retha, you can now enter the Holy of Holies. I have been waiting a long time for you to come.'*

What was supposed to be the worst day of my life turned out to be the best day, because that day, I met the King! And this is where deep calls unto deep, where spirit meets Spirit, where weakness is turned into strength, and mourning into dancing. The greatest treasure is to know Him and to be known by Him. In His presence you will find love, peace, acceptance, healing for a broken heart, and healing for a broken body. It is here, in this place, that I was overwhelmed by His goodness and felt Him smiling over His creation. I sensed how He loved the way He created me, even my curly hair that brings me so much frustration!

We have to realize that everything we will ever need is found in Him. There we will hear His heartbeat, and there He will reveal Himself to us. One second in His presence and my destiny changed forever! Finally, the veil over my eyes was removed.

'Father, please, I never want to lose this!' I said through my tears. I cried for the forty years, that I never knew there was more to my walk with God than just head-knowledge about

Him. There I realized I am His beloved daughter, not merely just a face in the crowd.

God spoke to me again and said, *'You could have been here a long time ago, but you were busy worshiping another god.'*

Taken aback, I replied, 'No, Lord. That can't be! I have been a Christian all my life!'

'My child, anything you love more than Me is an idol (see 1 John 5:21). It can be your job, your body, your husband; it can even be your children.'

(In my case, my children were definitely an idol in my life, but I am sad to say they weren't the only one.)

'Are you willing to offer your child to Me?'

Everything in me turned cold at His final question. Just as God asked it of Abraham, He asked it of me. He was asking me to sacrifice my Isaac. (Maybe He is even asking the same question of you today.) I realized I could not risk losing this precious gift of His presence, and that is why I gave God permission to have His way with Aldo. 'Yes, Lord. Take him. He belongs to You now.'

I realized then, that our priorities need to come in line with God's order: always God first, then our spouse, then our children, then our job. If we put God anywhere except right at the top of our list, we will never walk in the fullness of our divine purpose.

God says to all His children whose priorities are not in order: *'I am a jealous God and I have this against My children, that they have forsaken their first love. Remember therefore from where you have fallen; repent and do the first works'* (see Revelation 2:4-5).

God was definitely not my first love in the past. My children held that place, then my husband, then my job, and the last few minutes of the day belonged to God. Normally, I would be lying in bed by then asking God for all the things I thought I needed, and if He didn't respond in my prescribed time period, I would grumble.

Only after laying down my life before the King, was I allowed entrance into the Holy of Holies – the throne room of God. God's *shekinah* glory drenched the whole place. The first thing I wanted to do was to fall on my face before the King, and that is exactly what I did. I saw Aldo lying with me, and God's hand was stretched out toward him.

'I am going to raise up this child, and He will tell the world that Jesus is alive! He no longer belongs to you, he now belongs to Me; and you, My child, will have to walk the walk of faith. Faith is not what you see, but what you hope for. Remember, life is not about you, and from now on your lives belong to Me.'

To my shame, I thought to myself, 'But today is different, Lord. Today, it is about me. Just look at my child and see my broken heart!'

God knew my thoughts and answered, *'It is not even about your pain or heartache. At the end of the day, it is all about Me. You need to hand over everything in your life, so I can breathe My life into it. I let all things work together for the good of those who love Me and who are called according to My purpose'* (see Romans 8:28).

When I finally opened my eyes, almost two hours had passed by. I ran back to the ICU to find my son breathing on his own, even after they switched off the machines. Two hours earlier, we were planning for the worst, but now I had new hope, the God kind of hope – I had faith!

Even after they switched off the machines and Aldo breathed on his own, he was still in a coma for a long time and suffered a lot of pain. At long last he woke up, but his muscles were spastic and he couldn't eat, or walk, or talk. The doctors could do nothing more for him and we were given permission to take him home.

Through it all, we never stopped speaking life over him. As an act of faith, we started doing exercises with Aldo, and we firmly placed our hope in Jesus, believing that He would make him walk again.

Throughout this recovery process, there were many different kinds of therapists visiting him every day. One day, a therapist brought him the alphabet and a blank piece of paper. She encouraged him to draw on the paper, attempting to relieve some of the frustration he was dealing with. I silently sat and looked at the scenario playing off in front of me.

With a heart full of faith, I asked him, 'Aldo, do you want to write?' His head was drooping, but with the slightest movement of his head he indicated to me, in a way that only a mother could understand. Without saying a word, I heard a loud and clear, 'Yes, definitely Mom!' in my spirit.

I put the pen in his spastic hand and supported his palm with my hand. Slowly the movement started, and he wrote, 'Thank you, Mommy, that you gave me to Jesus. If you didn't do it, I would have been dead today.'

You can just imagine how I jumped up and down from excitement! How did he know that? He was in a coma, and I was on the other side of the ICU when that happened.

Later he wrote to me, 'Mommy, do you remember at the accident scene, while you were laying over me in the grass, you looked up into Jesus' eyes? He came and picked me up and took me to heaven with Him. He showed me heaven and hell. He was busy teaching me the entire time while we were in heaven. There were a lot of kids in heaven. I saw Moses and Abraham. The angels and everyone there were so happy, and nobody was sick.'

In another one of his letters he wrote:

Saf mamma asb alteyd vir Jesus werk ons weet dat Hy lewe want ons was by Jesus in die troonkamer

Hy gaan my 100% gesond
maak.
    gemaak soos klei
    maak God my
      'n nuwe mens
    uit Sy hand
tot Sy eer.
God sal my gebruik want ek is Sy
kind en sal Sy saam grootmaak
Eer God omdat ek lewe.

> *Will you please always work for Jesus, Mommy? We know that He is alive because we were both with Him in the throne room. He is going to heal me 100 percent. Like clay, God will form me into a new man with His hands, all for His honor. God will use me because I am His child and I will lift up His name. I honor God because I am alive!*

And this is how we started communicating with our son. For months, Aldo only wrote us letters, until we saw the next miracle taking place in front of our eyes: Aldo started talking! Very slowly, in monotone, he began conveying only his most basic needs, but it was the sweetest sound imaginable after months of silence.

Due to the nature of his injury, what he says doesn't always come out the way he intends and that is why he prefers to write when he has something important on his heart. We quickly learned that most mornings he has a message from God that he wants to write down. We bought him a journal to pen these messages each morning as the Holy Spirit imprinted them on his heart the previous night.

And so the first book, *A Message From God*, came to be. Aldo wrote about the children he saw in heaven, the houses, Moses, Abraham, and so much more. In the book the Bride of Christ is encouraged, and warned, to prepare herself for the return of the King, because He is coming soon.

Our family came to know a supernatural God with whom nothing is impossible. Aldo was sent back by God for a specific purpose. Aldo walks with God throughout the day, and at night Jesus takes him on heavenly journeys. Aldo saw heaven and hell, but mostly only wrote about heaven. When we asked him to write about hell, he would say, 'Jesus said at the right time He will talk about hell.'

Well, the time is at hand.

'Mommy, the time is now. Jesus is on His way. He says I must tell about what I saw in hell.' This is the reason for this book, *Heaven and Hell*, that you are now holding in your hands.

If you haven't read the first book, I would strongly encourage you to read it. You will experience the Holy Spirit in a fresh new way, and you will never be able to say you didn't know the truth. God uses a young boy, to once again, bring the message of His perfect love to His children.

Jesus paid the full price on the cross and that is why Aldo (even though he is not perfect in the world's eyes), can live a life of abundance just as Jesus promised. So too, for you and me:

> 'For God so loved the world
> that He gave His only begotten Son,
> that whoever believes in Him
> should not perish but have everlasting life.'
> *- John 3:16 -*

I want to start this book with the same words I started *A Message From God*...

'Know one thing for sure – Jesus is definitely alive!'

Tinus, Aldo, Retha, and Josh McPherson

Aldo – man of God, child at heart

God wys my bare groot
stadions waar ek gaan
bedien herlewing saam aan
mense sal werklik saam
kom gaan dan met
my eerste mense lewend
bid weet jy mamma god
se hy sal my nie het
so los nie god het vr
my weer gister nag self
gese ek het my eerste
preek gesien wat ek
hom al die eer gee. God
se ek het reeds wat
ek nodig het in my
mense sal werklik hom
het dadelik aanneem. god
het herhaal vir my gese
ek werk al reeds vir hom.
God mev wil jou seen
wees verseker werk en
weet jy het eendag n
groot groot verassing
wat god gese het saan
gebeur. God gaan dat pappa
saam ons bedien

> *God shows me many big stadiums where I am going to preach. There will be revival amongst the people.*
> *I will pray for the dead and they will arise.*
> *Do you know, Mommy, God says He won't leave me like this? God told me so Himself last night. I saw myself preaching my first sermon, and I gave Him all of the honor. God says I already have everything I need inside of me. People will really receive Him into their hearts immediately. God has told me repeatedly, I already work for Him. God wants to bless you Ma'am. Work for God and know for certain you have a big surprise from God waiting for you.*
> *God is going to let Daddy minister with us.*

Aldo is a walking miracle. If you had seen him during those first few brutal weeks in the ICU, and compare that picture to what he looks like now, I am sure you would agree with me.

In front of our eyes, Aldo changed from a twelve-year-old boy in a coma, to a young teenager with normal desires and needs. Like any other schoolboy, Aldo longs to be accepted by his friends and peers, and he enjoys doing the same 'teenager things' as others his age. Even though his spirit man has become a giant in this refining process, he is still a teenager at heart dealing with the growth pains of adolescence.

For the last four years, Josh and Aldo have been sleeping in a room that is connected to ours because Aldo had been sick most of the time. A normal day in our household starts at 4:00 A.M. with Aldo praying in his unique, and very loud, monotone voice. But for this mother who pled day and night with the Lord to open his spastic jaw, it is the sound of heaven! The only problem with Aldo's morning prayers is that once he is awake, all of us are awake. His prayers usually start something like this: 'Morning, God! Morning, Jesus! Morning, Holy Spirit!' On that note, we know a new day has dawned.

Praying has become second nature to Aldo. To him, praying is uncomplicated – it is simply talking to Jesus. Because he speaks so loudly, everybody in the house gets to listen to him praying. Believe me; it is quite an experience! These early morning hours have also become my own quiet time with the Lord, and our wake-up call is not a disturbance, but a blessing.

When Josh wakes up, he always declares, 'I am full of faith and controlled by the Holy Spirit!' (see Acts 6:5) I teach my children that a person can either be controlled by the Spirit or by the flesh, and Josh faithfully reminds me every morning. By making this declaration when he wakes up, Josh makes his choice before the day starts.

After praying, Aldo will jump up (usually at a pace too fast for his brain to process), and after falling down and trying a second time, he will start getting ready for school. He first has to finish his morning tasks, and then he will settle down to read his big-print Bible while waiting for his teacher, Miss Patrys, to pick him up.

For some reason he loves to read out of Genesis. I found this very strange, so one day I asked him why he only reads out of Genesis and never moves on. He answered, 'Everything we need to know comes from Genesis, Mom. Everything!'

Even though he struggles to read (because of his left eye-lid that is almost closed due to the nerve-injury), he somehow always finds his way back to Genesis. But, his knowledge of the Bible is not limited to the first book. Aldo will often quote other Scriptures from the rest of the Bible without reading them. His explanation for this is: 'Mommy, when I was in heaven, Jesus told me I will be working for Him here on earth. He wrote the entire Bible on my heart. I have already been to Bible school. Jesus taught me!'

my kweek skool gaan wees wat ek in die hemel gesien het. Jesus

27

wys my elke nag weer
en ek wil graag wees
sods ek daar was, gesond,

> My Bible school will be what I saw in heaven.
> Jesus shows it to me again every night.
> I want to be the same as I was there – healed!

Breakfast in our house is also not the same as in most other households and definitely never mundane. Over the years we have taught Aldo to eat with his left hand, because his right hand is often the reason for things being broken. Aldo's right arm is ataxic, and thus makes irregular and uncontrolled movements. Usually when Aldo starts talking, his right hand jumps into the air automatically. We have tried just about everything to manage his ataxia, but haven't found a solution yet. We tried scolding him, making him sit on his hand, and went so far as to bribe him with some sweets to keep his hand in his trouser pocket all day long. A spilled cool drink, or milkshake, is routine in a day at the McPherson household.

His hand also doesn't stay put during worship services at church, and every so often, it will venture into the hairdo of the lady sitting in front of us. Tinus has even tried playfully scolding him, 'Aldo, what are you going to do if the lady is wearing a wig? She is going to be very cross if her hairpiece falls to the ground! Please Aldo, put your hand in your pocket or hold onto the bench in front of you.'

At first, this was very frustrating and even a bit embarrassing. Later, the Lord reminded me of Moses, who had to keep his hands in the air in order for the army of Israel to defeat their foes. With this new perspective, our problem became a blessing and was no longer an embarrassment. With time, our family has learned to embrace and adapt to the uniqueness of our situation, and even to laugh at the obstacles we encounter.

For months after the accident, Aldo couldn't even open his mouth due to a spasm in his jaw. He had to receive his food through a tube to his stomach and he became very thin. I kept on pleading with the Lord to unlock his jaw, because I remembered what God told me in His throne room: *'This child will tell the world that Jesus is alive.'* God is not a man that He should lie, and He will not make empty promises (see Numbers 23:19). So I knew that in order for this promise to come to pass, Aldo would have to open his mouth, and that it would just be a matter of time.

One day, as I was walking through the airport on my way home from a speaking engagement, the Holy Spirit led me to buy sour-worm candy for Aldo. It was the kind he used to love before the accident. I placed one sweet into his mouth, day by day, for four days in a row, being aware of how risky this maneuver was. Miraculously, the sweets helped loosen his clenched jaw. I had no idea the sour candy would help with his locked jaw, I only wanted to relieve my son's pain, even if it was just with the small joy of tasting his favorite candy. God showed me how He can use anything to see His plans come to pass. We just need to obey the still small voice of the Holy Spirit inside of us, and not scorn the simplest of His commandments. Today I know that obedience to God leads us into holiness.

Now, like any other growing teenager, Aldo will often be found on his way to the fridge for something to eat. After all our prayers and petitions to get his jaw unclenched, you will never find me complaining about his healthy appetite! He still spills his drink occasionally, when he tries to use his right hand; but we have overcome that problem, too. We now only buy small cans rather than containers — problem solved!

The last thing Aldo normally does before leaving for school is to make a new entry in his journal. These journal entries are what Jesus told him the previous night. It usually includes a message from the Bridegroom to His Bride or a personal message to Tinus and me. Sometimes, he will even prophesy about a world event. Later, when we see these prophecies fulfilled, we stand amazed as we realize his letter was so spot on, even though he had no way of knowing.

Aldo's private tutor, Miss Patrys, picks him up at 7:15 A.M., and off they go to school. He attends a private school that works according to the Accelerated Christian Education (A.C.E.) system, where every student works at his own pace. Aldo and Miss Patrys have become very close, and she takes care of him with compassion and patience toward his special needs, as she would with her own son. Some days, they arrive at school, and Aldo will fall to his face to worship God before the bell rings, or he will start conversing with the angels around him. When this happens, you can try as you like, but you will not get him to give you his full attention. Miss Patrys gives him the freedom to do this. The school has a strong Christian foundation and the other kids and teachers also accept Aldo for who he is.

Break time is his favorite part of the day, because then he gets to play soccer with the rest of the kids. Before the accident, Aldo was my soccer star! He used to go to school early and wait for the gates to open, just so he could get a game in before school started.

It was hard getting used to the drastic change in our circumstances. In a blink of an eye, the rug was pulled from beneath our feet. I remember so clearly, standing at the end of his hospital bed, my heart aching as I remembered the days not so long ago when he used to run into the kitchen, soccer ball under his arm...only to be brought back to reality by the voices of the nurses and the beeps of the life support machine.

In my first encounter with God, His message was to speak life. That is exactly what I set out to do. 'Aldo, in Jesus' name, you will stand up from this bed to play soccer again with your friends!' The other patients and visitors gave us curious stares when Tinus and I spoke life over Aldo in such a passionate way. Considering the way he looked then, I can't say that I blame them. Regardless of what the world around me thought, I chose to believe God and to build my life, and the expectancy of my future, upon His Word.

I spoke to Aldo saying, 'Aldo, the Lord Himself will provide a Lamb for this burnt offering. Thank You, Jesus, that by Your stripes we are healed!' (See Genesis 22:8; Isaiah 53:5.)

There was no Plan B. Jesus was the only way out. He is the Way, the Truth, and the Life. If you are still holding on to a Plan B in your life, I want to tell you – you are wasting precious time. There is only one plan that works, and that plan is *Jesus!*

Not only did we speak words of life over Aldo's future, but we also acted upon our faith and started an intensive exercise program.

> 'For as the human body apart from the spirit is lifeless, so faith apart from [its] works of obedience is also dead.'
> - *James 2:26 AMP* -

Aldo's body was still stiff as a plank, but every day we picked him up out of his bed, and while Tinus held his upper body, I got down on my knees and moved his one foot in front of the other. Up and down the hall we would go. Because of these sessions in the hall and all my hours of praying, the hems of my skirts quickly became longer, as the scratch marks on my knees had to be covered. There was never a doubt in my mind that he would start walking again. The only question was, 'When?'

Giving up was never an option. We chose to replace those words in our vocabulary with *never stop*. Never stop trusting God. Never stop believing His Word. Never stop speaking words of life, and most importantly – never stop praising Him. Rather, persevere and endure! The harvest of our words did not come immediately, but we started seeing the fruit appear day by day as the years passed.

During that time, Aldo kept on writing: 'You will all see me walking one of these days, because Jesus is alive!' and, 'I will be healed because Jesus paid the full price for me.'

Even though we couldn't see any physical change immediately, we kept on confessing the Word and encouraging Aldo that he would play soccer with his friends again. That is what faith is: being assured of the things we hope for, the proof of the things we don't see (see Hebrews 11:1).

Finally, the day arrived when Aldo got out of his wheelchair and took his first shaky steps. He only took three steps and fell down again, but three steps were all we needed. Soon he had a lot of new bumps on his forehead as he practiced the art of walking. His arms still don't react fast enough to protect him when he falls, so these bumps just get worse and worse with time.

Today, almost five years later, we can see the reward of our seeds of faith. Aldo is playing soccer again! He is only the goalkeeper, but to this mom, he is (without a doubt) the best player on the field.

One day, he quietly came in after school and sat down on the couch, blankly staring out before him. After I spent a long time nagging, he finally came out with the reason for his somber expression: 'I wasn't chosen for the school team, Mom.' I sat down next to him to comfort him, but found that I didn't have any words. I knew all too well why they didn't choose him. The kids let him play goalie during break to make him feel part of the group, but for a match he wouldn't be the best choice. He can still only walk a few steps before losing his balance, and running is out of the question. My seventeen-year-old son is constantly confronted with *not being good enough*.

'Aldo, my darling, you know you weren't sent back to play on the school team. God has big plans for your life. He sent you back to tell the world that Jesus is alive. Never take your focus off your calling. All the rest will fall into place.'

In my mind, a thousand thoughts suddenly surface while I am sitting next to him on the couch. I remember what he looked like in ICU, the negative reports when they told me he would never walk again, how we prayed for his spastic jaw, and his first steps, and how we exercised up and down the hall – and I think to myself, 'God is good and faithful. My son is alive and playing soccer again! If not being chosen for the school team is our biggest problem, we are blessed indeed!'

I look at him with eyes that see past the cuts and bumps on his face, past his hanging left eye, and I give him my best smile and a wink: 'You are playing soccer again, Aldo!' Slowly he replies, 'Yes, but there is much more in me than only goalie.' I can only laugh, and then try to distract him with a cool drink.

On the evening of his disappointment over the soccer team, I realized that, after a long while, Aldo still hadn't come out of the bathroom. I walked in to check on him and as he tried to get out, he slipped and fell. With a big splash, he ended up on the floor, hitting his head hard. Suddenly, there was blood everywhere. I screamed loudly, 'Tinus, quickly. Come help!' Within minutes, we were on our way to the hospital and returned an hour later with Aldo covered in stitches. And so a typical day, full of unforeseen challenges, came to an end.

Finally, everything settled down in our house as everyone was off to bed. Little Josh climbed onto my lap and whispered, 'Mommy, will you please tickle my back? But only if you want to.'

I gave him a kiss, prayed for him, and gave in to his request. The God kind of peace that transcends all understanding once again covered all of us.

Everything around me was quiet; only from Aldo's room did I still hear a sound. 'Aldo, are you OK?' After all this time, Aldo still can't cry and only makes a crying sound when he's sad. My heart broke for him that night, because I realized he is trapped in his body, with no way to express himself. I tried to get him to talk to me, but he simply didn't want to. Aldo still struggles to get his thoughts and his words to coincide, and he sometimes says the wrong thing at the wrong time.

'Please leave me now, Mom. I want to go with Jesus.'

I held on to the fact that God would fully restore my child, but at the same time, I understood the frustration Aldo was dealing with at that moment. My constant prayer to God, every day of my life, is that He will bring Aldo's spirit, soul, and flesh in line with His Word.

Wens so ek kan soos almal wees Luister asb na God se stem want nou is god werklik besig om met sy bruid te praat. Wie sal gehoorsaam wees aan sy stem? Weet asb altyd ons is uitgekies vir u. Jesus se ons gaan minder ~~ons~~ word en Hy meer.

> I wish I was like everybody else.
> Please listen to God's voice,
> because God is busy talking to His Bride.
> Who will be obedient to His voice?
> Please know, we are handpicked by Jesus.
> Jesus says we will become less and He will become more.

'Goodnight everyone,' he said that night. 'I am going to Jesus now' and with those words the family slumbered in. The next morning, Aldo would wake up and write down what Jesus showed him in his dreams the night before.

I can't wait for each morning to break, just so I can read his latest letter.

Aldo finds all his comfort in the Lord. For him, there is no other way. Only Jesus fully understands what He is going through. At night, I close my eyes and see how all four of us are covered by the blood of the Lamb and drenched in His Holy Spirit.

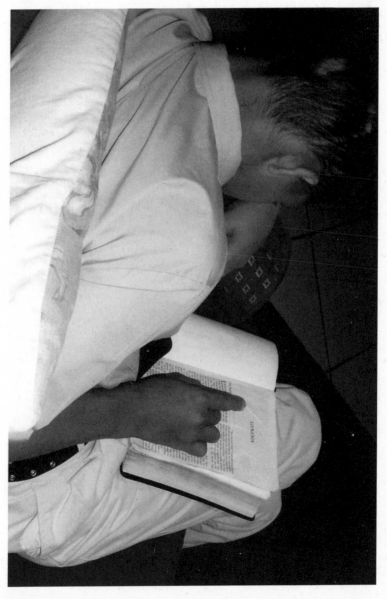

Walking by faith and not by sight

Jesus se ek sal jou gesond wees mense sal jou bel en era wat moet huilt doen. God sal my gesond maak. het jy werk vir my ek sal my getuienis vertel wat ek gesien het in die hemel en die hel. Jy sal moet werk. want weet het wat ek van weet hoor ek het by die Heilsige gees. God se sy Gees sal my altyd leer.

Jesus says I will be healed soon.
People will phone you to ask what they must do.
God will heal me. Do you have a job for me?
I will tell my testimony of what I saw in heaven and hell.
You must work and you must know that everything
I know I hear from the Holy Spirit.
God says His Spirit will always teach me.

Aldo started writing letters as a means of communication. For months after the accident he couldn't speak one word, but we improvised and helped him to write. Some of his letters were very basic, mostly only communicating his needs: 'hungry', 'thirsty', 'Jesus will heal me' and lots and lots of 'faith in God, faith in God, faith in God'.

He also wrote of how Jesus picked him up after the accident and took him to heaven. He wrote about everything he saw in heaven and some of the things he saw in hell. He wrote about the angels, Moses, Abraham, and all the other children he met and played with in heaven. In one of his letters he wrote:

> *We will see God in heaven with all the angels and other people like Abraham and Moses. Dwane and Anton will also be there. Look forward with me to going back.*
> *I am so difficult because I want to go back.*
> *Will you tell people, they either go to heaven or hell?*
> *The children of the devil will go to hell but God's children will go to heaven.*
> *As God lives, so will we live in heaven.*
> *We will go to Jesus. Look forward to it!*

We were surprised to see the spiritual wisdom flowing from such a seemingly broken vessel. Nonetheless, we started drinking from the pure living water brought to us through his letters – it is Aldo's spirit man talking to us through these letters. From the Scriptures contained in the letters, we could see that his spirit man is one with the Holy Spirit. One day I asked him again, 'Aldo, how do you know all these Scriptures?' and he reminded me that Jesus wrote the whole Bible on his heart while he was in heaven.

These *heavenly letters* were very strange to us. Tinus and I were church goers before the accident, but we didn't know much about the supernatural or miracles. I soon realized that the flesh cannot justify or explain the things of the Spirit, and that is why *faith* is so important. Through our faith-eyes we can look at our situation from God's perspective and know that our greatest 'impossibility' is a small thing for the Creator of the universe, for with God nothing is impossible!

Initially, I didn't want to tell anybody from the outside world of these messages from God. I could just imagine what the people would say. Even till today, I see how people want to figure this out with their minds. Our carnal minds cannot fathom the limitlessness of God's might, His power, and His greatness. God can do whatever He wants, how He wants. His miracles are limitless.

As time went by, the messages became more and more intense and prophetic. We could clearly see that Aldo was writing of things he could not possibly have known about in the natural. As he matured, his letters evolved. Lately, when he writes, he will always refer to the Holy Spirit as *Wisdom*.

> For the Lord gives skillful and godly Wisdom,
> from His mouth come knowledge and understanding.
> *- Proverbs 2:6 AMP -*

Luister na alles wat
Wysheid se. god gee
my die kennis. god weet
jy sal hooit opgee nie.

> *Listen to everything Wisdom says. God gives me
> the knowledge. God knows you will never give up.*

During the time when Aldo was still unable to talk, I received a strange phone call one morning, while dropping Josh off at school. It was lady who was concerned about our situation, after she read an article in the newspaper. She said, 'Retha, I read that after four months, your son still can't talk. I know of a doctor from Germany who specializes in cell-membrane transplants. Don't you want to schedule a consultation? Maybe it will help.' I told her that I would discuss it with my family, but Jesus had already promised to heal my child, and I would only be able to give her an answer after praying about it.

When I walked back into the house, I could see Aldo was upset. As we sat down to journal, he wrote, 'Mommy, Jesus will let me talk again. Jesus, and only Jesus, will get the honor.'

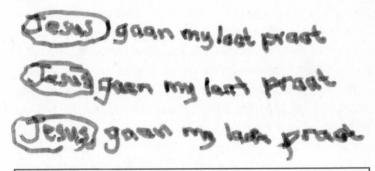

> Jesus will make me speak
> Jesus will make me speak
> Jesus will make me speak

I was totally confused and wondered how it was possible for him to know about the conversation I had while dropping Josh off? I ran to my study, fell to my knees, and prayed: 'Jesus, please talk to me. How does Aldo know all these things without anybody telling him about them?'

The Holy Spirit responded with a soft voice to my heart, 'Retha, he walks in the Spirit. He sees, hears, and lives in the Spirit. This is My desire for all My children, to move past the things which are temporal and live in the realm of things which are eternal' (see 2 Corinthians 4:18).

Aldo's spiritual senses are alert and focused on God. This godly privilege to live in the Spirit and to hear the voice of

Wisdom so clearly is there for all of us. God, who is the Creator of creativity, speaks to His children in many different ways. He can use nature, visions, dreams, prophets, His Word, and the conviction of His Spirit to name a few. To hear the voice of His Spirit, we must first of all be filled with the Holy Spirit, and then consciously tune our hearing to His voice.

I have found that God often uses visions or pictures to speak to me. The descriptions I give below are by no means fixed doctrine; I am only trying to explain in my own words how I understand it: A prophetic 'inner-vision' or 'impression' will typically be a picture you see with the eyes of your heart. A 'night vision' is when God speaks to you through your dreams, when your outer man is relaxed and won't reason against what God is trying to show you. 'Open visions' occur when you are completely awake and aware of what is going on around you in the natural, but your spiritual eyes see beyond the veil like a movie being played out in front of you (see Acts 10:10-16). Lastly, 'participating visions' or 'trans visions' involve your active participation in the vision. There are many great men of God who shared in this privilege of participating visions, like Daniel, Ezekiel, and the disciple John (see Daniel 10:5-8, Ezekiel 37:1-10, Revelation 1:10).

Likewise, Jesus visits Aldo at night while he sleeps and even travels with Him to different places around the world. In the mornings, Aldo writes about their journeys.

> *I was in heaven again last night with Jesus.*
> *Jesus showed me my house. He showed me again there are few who enter heaven. Jesus says I am ready because I have accepted Him and laid down my life for Him.*

I didn't always understand the spirit realm or these supernatural experiences; and at times, my natural mind still does not fully comprehend what God is doing with Aldo. However, the longer I walk by faith and not by sight the more I understand, because my spirit becomes stronger in the Lord.

With Aldo in our house, we experience the reality of the spiritual realm firsthand in our day-to-day life. What is hindering most of us from experiencing the supernatural wonders of God, is that our thoughts are held captive by what we see. We will not be able to enter into the deeper things of the Spirit with our carnal minds or our flesh. We all need to pray and ask God to open our spiritual senses to Him, so we can worship Him, spirit to Spirit.

'Now we have received, not the spirit of the world,
but the Spirit who is from God,
that we might know the things that have been freely given
to us by God. These things we also speak,
not in words which man's wisdom teaches
but which the Holy Spirit teaches,
comparing spiritual things with spiritual.
But the natural man does not receive the things of
the Spirit of God, for they are foolishness to him;
nor can he know them,
because they are spiritually discerned.
But he who is spiritual judges all things,
yet he himself is rightly judged by no one.
For "who has known the mind of the LORD that he may instruct Him?"
But we have the mind of Christ.'
- 1 Corinthians 2:12-16 -

Through Aldo's life, you will see that the spiritual realm is more real to him than the natural realm. For example, he will be sitting at the dinner table and then something happening in the spirit realm will catch his attention. He will then get so involved with whatever is happening in the supernatural, that he won't even touch his food.

I remember so clearly when he jumped up one evening and said into the atmosphere, 'What should I call you?'

We all asked almost simultaneously, 'To whom are you speaking, Aldo?'

Confused, he replied, 'Can't you see him? He is such a big angel! Listen carefully, maybe you will hear him move.'

At another time, Tinus and I were sitting in the living room watching television, while Aldo was already in bed. The next moment, he stumbled into the room and asked which one of us called him.

'No, Aldo. No one called you, but you can come and sit with us for a little while before going to bed again.'

Knowingly, he replied, 'No, no, I'd rather go to bed... if it wasn't you, it can only be Jesus. Goodnight.'

Hastily, he returned to bed. Later, I walked in to see him lying on his back, fast asleep with his hands intertwined as when praying. I just knew he was away with Jesus somewhere, and I would have to wait until morning for his letter to know what happened on their journey.

Right then, I knelt before his bed. 'Jesus, I still have so much to learn. Thank You, Holy Spirit, that You are my Teacher!'

Events such as these built my faith tremendously. With a heart full of expectancy, I drew closer and closer to God, hoping to taste these supernatural experiences myself. I knew God would open my spiritual eyes at the right time, but my spirit-capacity had to be big enough to accept what God wanted to show me.

Jesus was gister aag hier
Luister na sy stem

Jesus was here last night. Listen to His voice.

Today, I know the reason why I couldn't always see what Aldo saw: my flesh was still ruling over my spirit. My carnal mind would reason against the supernatural, before it could be established in my spirit (like the birds that devoured the seeds in Matthew 13). We need to always remember that

God's Kingdom is not flesh and blood, but spirit. We need to fill up our spirit with seeds of truth from the Word. Only once the truth is firmly rooted in our being, will we be able to walk by faith and not by sight.

> *Jesus says we will experience His power in*
> *everything we do. Like last night, it will only increase.*
> *Only seek His presence and all the rest shall be added to you.*
> *Will you always place God first in your life?*
> *I will preach His Word all the days of my life.*
> *God is all we need. We are seeking His presence.*
> *Please be ready when He comes to fetch us.*
> *I love Jesus with all my heart and He loves me too.*

More than ever, I can say we serve a supernatural God with whom nothing is impossible. If we walk by faith, we can walk on water.

Thank You, Jesus, that walking on water is safer than staying in the boat – because You are waiting for us on the water!

my wil my sy
Liefde gee elke dag. Wysheid
wil my leer sal my self
leer wat werklik noe gaan
hy weer kom hy is oppad
wysheid leer my wat ek
weet. ek skryf net wat
wysheid se ek moet skryf

> *God wants to give me His love every day.*
> *Wisdom teaches me what I know.*
> *I only write what Wisdom says I must write.*

Do you know Ma'am, Wisdom Himself came
and told me what He wants me to write?

The Lion of Judah in me

Jy is Jesus se kind ek en jy
gaan bedien my God het
my die hemel gewys
het jy geweet hy se hy
weet hoe swaar ek kry
Lief vir jou
Wys my hoe het ek gelyk
voor die Ongeluk
Weet jy ek wens so
ek kan julle weer gelukkig
maak. Jesus se my God sal
my gesond maak. God se
ek wil werk want wat hy
my gewys het. Lewe was
het ek sal vir hom werk

Leeu van Juda

You are Jesus' child and you and I are going to preach
together. God showed me heaven and He said He knew how
difficult it is for me (here on earth). I love you, Mommy.
Show me how I looked before the accident.
I wish I could make you happy again. Jesus says my God will
heal me. God says I want to work for Him.
He showed me true life. I will work for Him – Lion of Judah.

Aldo enjoyed a very typical life before the accident. He went to Sunday school, had fun on his quad bike over weekends, played soccer with his friends, and just enjoyed the usual carefree pleasures of youth. Like any other twelve-year-old, Playstation video games and watching television were a large part of his daily activities. When I stood at his hospital bed, I realized of how little value some of these activities were. With regret in my heart, I knew I couldn't buy back the lost time.

When Aldo awoke from the coma, we received a new son. God sent him back as a boy who had died to himself and whose life was now hidden in Christ (see Colossians 3:3). His perspective about himself and the world around him was totally different from what we were used to. His mission was clear: He must be the hands and feet of Jesus and carry the light into dark places with three simple words, *Jesus is alive!*

Jy en ek sal gaan en saam god se woord verkondig

> *You and I will go, and together we will preach God's Word!*

Aldo still struggles with his fleshly nature, just like you and me, but His spirit cries out for holiness. He was sent back to live a life separated unto God. This is the path *all* Christians should walk, not just those who have had supernatural experiences. If we want to be overcomers, we can't afford the luxury of being lukewarm (the overcomers are the citizens of heaven described in Revelation 2 and 3).

The new Aldo is dramatically different from the old Aldo, and it took some time getting used to. Not only Aldo, but all the members of our family had to lay down their lives, pick up their crosses, and follow Jesus. That meant we had to turn our backs on the carnal life we lived up to that point, and start walking in the Spirit, with our focus only on Jesus.

The new Aldo walks two steps and stumbles three, but they are guided by the Holy Spirit. He talks in a slow monotone voice, but his words carry a message that needs to be heard. Aldo rarely complains, and he doesn't allow these setbacks to hinder him. The new Aldo *lives and moves and has his being in Jesus* (see Acts 17:28).

What *does* bother him, is when people finish his sentences for him or turn around without giving him a chance to speak. Like all of us, he wants to be acknowledged, accepted, and respected. He takes on any challenge and his hand is usually first in the air when his teachers are looking for volunteers. I am constantly surprised by his brave heart! Aldo honestly believes that he has strength for all things through Christ who empowers him (see Philippians 4:13).

Some days, when I look at his outside condition, I secretly wonder to myself how he will be able to preach. The enormity of the miracle-in-waiting tempts to overwhelm me when I lose sight of the greatness of the God we serve. It is then that I fall to my knees and pray this one prayer: "Father, please let his spirit, soul, and flesh come into perfect alignment with Your Word."   As peace floods my soul again, I rest in the fact that God is God. The foundations of His throne are righteousness and justice, and no matter what happens on earth, He will always be on the throne! Almighty. Sovereign. Completely in control. This is my God. His ways of how He will use His son are always the best, for He sees the bigger picture and He knows what the future holds.

In another one of his letters Aldo wrote:

> *Mommy, I will be obedient to Jesus.*
> *He says I must work for Him and preach His Word.*
> *Will you please help me? You must know, Mommy,*
> *you and I will preach His Word together.*

In Aldo's school, all the teachers and students assemble every Friday morning to pray and prophecy as the Spirit of the

Lord leads them. The teachers do this to train the children in the spiritual gifts, and to equip a new generation as soldiers for Jesus.

On a sunny Friday morning, a little girl from the first grade stood up and prophesied over Aldo: 'Jesus shows me you are a big lion walking around in a cage. He is keeping you safe and separated in this cage until the day He wants to let you out.'

When Miss Patrys told me this story, I immediately ran for his journal. Her words reminded me of a letter Aldo wrote a long time ago. After searching a few minutes, I found the letter I was looking for:

gediening totdat my h ae ny mq wegsteek tot wanneer ek gereed is om te bedien.

> *He shows me how He hides me*
> *until it is time for me to preach.*

> For in the time of trouble He shall hide me
> in His pavilion; In the secret place of His tabernacle
> He shall hide me; He shall set me high upon a rock.
> *- Psalm 27:5 -*

We serve a faithful God! He knew all our days before we took one breath, and He knew about this confirmation, long before Aldo wrote the letter. I couldn't help but rejoice at this double-confirmation, because Jesus says the Kingdom of God belongs to the little children! (see Luke 18:16.)

Another example of Aldo's never-give-up outlook on life is his passion for sports. He is convinced he can be a very good athlete, even if he can't run a hundred meters without falling!

As the bell rings to indicate the start of athletic practice, the children slowly and lethargically wind their way to the track – but not Aldo. Miss Patrys needs to quicken her step to keep up with him. Even when the track is wet and covered in mud, Aldo doesn't see this as an excuse not to give his best. He pulls loose from Miss Patrys' grip, and with all of his strength, he starts running around the field. Aldo can't even walk properly, so I hope you can anticipate what is coming! In his awkward manner, he runs (or more accurately falls) around the track. The rest of the teachers and students watch his audacity in a stunned silence.

Covered in mud, but with a proud grin on his face, he tells us of his day when he comes home. Privately, I wonder to myself if he even realizes he can't run, and so one day, I responded, 'Aldo, Daddy will buy you a weight tomorrow so you can also participate in the athletics, but rather try your best in the shot-put event. Leave the running to the other children. You will only get hurt.'

Slowly but surely he said, 'No, Mommy. I am also an athlete. God knows my potential. You only see my outside. Don't look at me through your flesh eyes, Mom. Look at me through God's eyes.' He stood up, indicating the end of the conversation, and went to his room.

To him, he had won the prize that day, and he slept with the sweet assurance that he had given his best. He won a golden medal in God's Kingdom!

Long after such conversations, I lie awake and think about his words. I ask the Holy Spirit to help me see through God's eyes, and suddenly I see a completely new picture: Yes, all of us are running a race of life. The race is in the Spirit and the prize is an imperishable crown. There is a great reward for victory, but also a terrible price for defeat.

Do you not know that those who run in a race all run, but one receives the prize? Run in such a way that you

> may obtain it. And everyone who competes for the
> prize is temperate in all things.
> Now they do it to obtain a perishable crown,
> but we for an imperishable crown.
> Therefore I run thus: not with uncertainty…
> *- 1 Corinthians 9:24-25 -*

Only those who keep to the rules will win the prize. The victor's crown of life is reserved for those who through faith and patience attain God's promises (see Hebrews 6:12). If we want to win, we don't have the luxury of self-pity, excuses, or blaming others. We can't look around to see how others are doing it. We need to do the best with whatever God has entrusted us with. We need to stay focused on our race and the ultimate prize. We need to run with all of our strength towards Jesus. Nothing else will do.

Today, I know God will match His assignment for your life with your unique character, your abilities, your obedience, and your love relationship with Him. What you do with the portion God has given you…that is up to you.

Lewe soos Jesus wys in sy woord. Wys mense dat Jesus lewe

Live like Jesus shows us in His Word.
Show people that Jesus is alive!

A lonely road

het jy geweet ek wil nie
so wees nie my hart
is seer oor my lewe
wat so vreeslik eensaam
is. God sien alles
en hy se ek weet wat
wag het jy geweet my
maats het my almal
gelos want ek is nou
heeltemal anders hulle
besef nie ek is net
Aldo nie wens hulle
kan sien wat ek sien.
hulle weet nie eers Jesus
is oppad nie. het jy
my lief net soos ek is.
ek sal julle nie teleurstel
nie. Jy verstaan nie my
wens is net om julle
gelukkig te maak. weet jy
my kop is nou heeltemal reg.
wil net nou regkom het
hou net my lewe gesien.
Lewe vir Jesus

> *Do you know I don't want to be like this?*
> *My heart is breaking because my life is so lonely.*
> *God sees everything and He says I know what is waiting. Did*
> *you know all my friends left me*
> *because I am so much different than them?*
> *They don't realize I am just Aldo. I wish they could see what I*
> *see. They don't even know Jesus is on His way.*

> *Do you love me just the way I am?*
> *I won't disappoint you, Mommy. Don't you understand it is*
> *my desire to make you happy again?*
> *My head is feeling much better. Live only for Jesus.*

Shortly after we brought Aldo home from the hospital, the lovely teacher from his previous school arranged for the year-end class party to be held at our home to include Aldo in the fun. Grownups and children tried their best to act normal, but I could see the awkwardness reflected on their faces in the strained atmosphere. While the rest of the children splashed in the pool, Aldo could only sit as an observer in his wheelchair. His head was drooping to one side, body still spastic, and worst of all, he was silent because of his locked jaw. Not being able to talk built an invisible wall between him and the outside world.

After everyone left, he spoke to me through his journal:

> *Jesus says we will preach His Word together*
> *and the seminar you are going to give about*
> *the Holy Spirit will be successful. Jesus will anoint us,*
> *so we can anoint others with His Holy Spirit.*
> *God says we will be ready. Will you tell others*
> *they must be ready when Jesus comes to fetch us?*
> *Some of my friends aren't ready. Will you help me pray*
> *for them that they can also go to heaven?*
> *Jesus wants to use me to pray for them.*
> *Like us, they will also offer their lives to God.*

Tears stained the paper as I read this letter. I knew God had irrevocably changed my son and that nothing would ever be the same again.

All of his friends disappeared one by one as time went by, all except one – Bradley. Bradley could look beyond Aldo's spastic body and crooked smile to see the treasure hidden in the clay pot.

Every Friday after school, Bradley would ring our doorbell and ask ever so politely, 'Good afternoon, Ma'am. Is Aldo here?'

Laughingly, I would reply 'Of course, Bradley. He is down the hall in his room.' Both Bradley and I knew Aldo wouldn't be anywhere else.

Today, five years later, Bradley still comes to visit, but now mostly on Sunday afternoons. Bradley and Aldo will play soccer together, or shoot games of pool, or just lay in the sun beside the swimming pool and chat. Bradley patiently listens to Aldo as Aldo tells him of his new school. I hear Bradley laugh at Aldo's questions of the outside world, and his questions about girls.

On Valentine's Day, on his way to the car, Aldo picked a garden rose for a girl at school, but he received a cool reply. He was very quiet that afternoon and stared at himself in the mirror. 'Is it because of my eye, Mommy?' he wanted to know. I pulled him into a bear hug to keep myself from crying, and little Josh came to our rescue. "Aldo, you need to focus. Jesus has a special girl in the palm of His hand for you. Don't settle for anything less than God's best. Just wait for her!'

With this encouragement from his younger brother, he waggled to his room, fell on his knees, and has waited on God. Only God can give him the peace and love he so desperately craves.If God has destined you to be married, He has already handpicked the person you are going to spend the rest of your life with. We need to keep ourselves pure for this amazing gift from God. I don't encourage dating – I believe in friendship. If God wants it to be anything more than that, He will bring it to pass. I often tell Aldo that God is preparing an amazing woman to be his wife; he just needs to be patient.

Yes, there is life after tragedy: school from 8 A.M. to 2 P.M., afternoons with his teacher and caretaker Miss Patrys, and evenings with the family. Unfortunately, there is not much socializing with friends to fill the gaps.

One afternoon, the two of us were playfully wrestling, and I was laughing a lot at Aldo's antics. Afterwards, as we lay on the bed, he confided to me the longing in his heart for his friends that were once such a large part of his life. That night, he wrote the letter you read at the beginning of this chapter: *Do you know I don't want to be like this? My heart is breaking because my life is so lonely…*

As I read the letter I thought to myself, 'Of course I know you don't want to be like this, my love. My heart is breaking, too…' One evening Aldo kept on making the crying sound for a long time, and then he wrote:

Dear Mommy, I feel much better. Do you love me?
Know for certain my wisdom comes from God.
I wish I could have my old friends back. They all left me.
Do you have a better life now? …Because I do.
Jesus says the reason I am crying is for a lost world.

His letter describes the warring between flesh and spirit. Our flesh wants things easy and comfortable, but our spirit knows that to walk in the abundant life of Christ, we need to die daily to our fleshly cravings.

'Therefore, since Christ suffered for us in the flesh,
arm yourselves also with the same mind,
for he who has suffered in the flesh has ceased from sin,
that he no longer should live the rest of his time
in the flesh for the lusts of men, but for the will of God.'
- *1 Peter 4:1-2* -

On the one hand we have those friends who avoid Aldo, and on the other hand we have those visitors who are only interested in what they can get from Aldo – people seeking a word from God or a prophecy. Parents want to arrange play-dates for their children with Aldo just to hear what he has to say. I shrink away from such invitations, because I sense the motive for the friendship is not pure. Sometimes I feel like screaming: 'Please, Aldo is not a fortune-teller!'

> *You are right. I am inside.*
> *Do you know how badly I want to get out?*
> *Yes, I know I will get out. I also know my wife is keeping herself pure. God wants to teach you what faith is.*
> *Just know I love you very much. Thank you very much that you and I can laugh together. Do you know what I miss the most is to laugh with my friends.*
> *Do you know that what I want to say and what comes out of my mouth are not always the same?*

My son is, at his core, only a teenager with a human heart. Like your child, he is also looking for friends who will love him for who he is and not for what he can give them. Aldo needs a safe place where he will have the liberty to be himself without judgment or criticism. A place where he can learn and grow in his human relationships in the same way the rest of us do – by making mistakes and learning from them. He needs the unconditional kind of friendship, and sometimes I wonder if that kind still exists.

Then there is Eric. He is a few years older than Aldo and befriended Aldo in the A.C.E school where they both attended. He has already graduated, but Aldo longingly remembers his compassionate heart and helping hands. With the older and wiser Eric, he felt comfortable to share his heart. 'Eric, how do you kiss a girl?' or 'Are boys allowed to look at girls?' and after a long pause 'But how long is looking *too* long, Eric?'

Eric attended Aldo's school awards ceremony at the end of 2008, and he was a great support to his old friend simply by being in the crowd. Aldo felt so proud knowing Eric was there cheering him on. When Aldo received his prize, he looked to see if Eric was watching and lifted his thumb triumphantly in his direction. It was a great loss when Eric graduated and started his career. What he meant to Aldo in that season of friendship is priceless and will never be forgotten.

A sweet girl, who knows Aldo's story, arranged that the two of them, accompanied by her mom, Miss Patrys, and some other friends, go out for a milkshake one Friday afternoon. The night before the meeting, the rest of the family (all of us being a bit nervous) gave him tips on how to behave, as we sat around the dinner table. Josh explained, by acting it out, how to greet her as a gentleman with the hand.

The afternoon of their meeting I was out of town, and I had to wait until evening to find out how it went. Miss Patrys explained in detail: 'Aldo enjoyed it so much! After they got to know each other, and chatted a while, he got up and bought both of them a soft-serve ice cream. Wiggle-waggle he walked back to the table and handed her the ice cream (this already surprised me, because he has a lot of difficulty walking on his own). He made it to the table, and thankfully the ice cream found its way to her hand without a mess. After they enjoyed the ice cream, she stood up, got a serviette, and wiped his mouth clean.'

When Miss Patrys got to this part of the story, I couldn't stop the tears any longer. 'Oh, Jesus, please bless that precious girl; bless her Lord!' From her humble actions, I can see the heart of the King.

We are not only trusting God for Aldo's complete healing and restoration, but also for those divinely appointed friends, and even his wife, who will love the imperfect – *perfectly*. She will be handpicked by God. One of a kind. Unique. Priceless. Just like Aldo.

Laat jou begeertes aan god bekend word,

> *Let your desires be made known to God.*

Jesus, I thank You for Your great grace towards us. Thank You that those who believe will see the glory of God.

Thank You that not one of Your promises will be left unfulfilled. Thank You for Aldo's healing, for his friends, and for his wife. Thank You, Jesus, that we can pour out our hearts before You and thank You, Lord, that You hear our prayers. Thank You that You are always with us, and we are never alone. You are worthy to be praised, and I love You with all my heart.

God gives all of us the invitation to trust Him for the things that would be utterly impossible if we had to attempt them on our own.

Put your trust in God – He is faithful!

'For with God nothing will [ever] be impossible.'
- Luke 1:37 -

Bradley and Aldo

Eric and Aldo

Miss Patrys

Liewe Suf Patrys
weet asb ek is
baie lief vir jou.
Jy het werklik vir
my wereld kom help
weet ek werk vir Jesus
werk saam my asb.
wysheid en ek werk
wysheid wys my werk
www.aldomcpherson.com
god het jou gekies
hy se ek en sy gaan
bid vir mense gaan
weer skool gaan
tot volgende jaar hy
wys my Jy het hom
gevra wat word van
jou ny se Jy sal
saam my werk waar
wysheid my huisbou
hy wys my ek en
ny wysheid het hemel
vertel vir mense. god se
ny weet Jy kry nog seer
hy en Heilige gees hou jou
vertrou hom ek weet
wie hom liefhet sal hy nie
los nie

> *Dear Miss Patrys,*
> *Please know I love you very much.*
> *You have come to help me in this world.*
> *Know I am working for Jesus. Please work with me.*
> *Wisdom and I work together.*
> *Wisdom shows me I need to work.*
> *God has chosen you. He says you and I are going*
> *to pray for people. I will be in school until next year.*
> *He showed me you asked Him what is going to happen*
> *to you after I am finished with school.*
> *He said you will work with me where Wisdom is*
> *building my house. He shows me that Wisdom and*
> *I will tell the people of heaven.*
> *God says He knows you are still hurting.*
> *He and the Holy Spirit are holding you tightly.*
> *Trust Him.*
> *I know He will never let go of those who love Him.*

Have you ever heard the term 'go-getter'?

I am sure you can think of a few people who fall into that category. Maybe you would even be so bold as to describe yourself by this term. Now, dear friends, try and put Aldo's life in context by considering the obstacles he faces daily.

Many of us don't reach, or even eagerly pursue, our goals when we have everything we need at our disposal to achieve them. We have the freedom to move around easily without assistance and speak clearly to give voice to our thoughts. Most of us have no handicap, yet we may lack passion, determination, and the will to succeed.

Aldo, on the other hand, is full of cuts and bruises to show for his determined and brave heart. Time after time Aldo falls to the ground when his natural disability hinders his passion. Falling down is never an excuse for him to stay down. He will always get back up again.

I have a God-given assignment to be the teacher of a young man who gives new meaning to the word 'go-getter'! Once Aldo has put his mind to something; believe me, nothing will stop him from accomplishing his goal.

When the other healthy students in his school are still wondering whether they want to participate in an event, Aldo is already chasing after the prize. He will do whatever it takes to complete the task set before him. If they need a volunteer for a school activity, Aldo's hand is first to go up. If we exercise and he needs to do ten repetitions, he will say, 'No, fifteen!' With this determination to succeed, he tackles everything in life. In the four years of being his teacher, I have never heard him say he can't do it. *Impossible* is just not in his vocabulary.

Recess is his favorite part of the day. He closely keeps an eye on his watch not to miss a second of it. To run around with his friends on the rugby field is a dream come true for him. He prizes friendship very highly and always remembers the names of the new children in school, no matter what age they are. One of his classmates, Nathan, played a game with him the other day and Aldo was bent over with laughter. While other kids take it for granted, friendship is a most precious gift to him.

Aldo's motto for life is to give everything he attempts his best shot. All-out work, all-out play, and, naturally, all-out Jesus!

His relationship with God is characterized by his innocent honesty. The other day, he prayed for another teacher who was feeling a bit sick. He asked, 'Lord, please heal her, but don't take too long. Please, Jesus. Please heal her today!'

Aldo talks to God throughout the entire day. He falls down on his knees next to his desk or throws his hands together and gives the Lord praise regardless of what we are busy with. He will send up a plea to God anywhere, anyplace. When driving, he opens the window of the car an inch and then talks to the Lord through the crack in the window. When I interrupt these conversations, he sometimes says, 'Excuse me, Lord. I have to go now.' On other occasions, he tells me he can't speak to me now, because it is more important to finish his conversation with God first.

I daily praise my heavenly Father for the privilege of seeing how He turns every tear, every hurt, and every thorn in the flesh into a testimony for His glory!

Because of Aldo, I have learned to say 'thank you' when tested. Through the tests, we learn of what great measures God takes to mold and shape us.

Because of his special needs, Aldo's wings have been clipped. But by God's grace, He has taught him a new way to fly. He glides like an eagle on the holy presence of the Lord.

As we drive to school, his favorite song to sing is *'You Raise Me Up'.*

I can't help but think how beautiful the sound of his song must be to the Lord.

Miss Patrys

The school of His Spirit

My hart is so seer
so groot want ek is 16
vandag   Weet jy mamma
wat jy vir my doen wardeer
ek so baie. Wysheid sal
jy ontvang om my te help.
Weet ek sal self skryf
baie boeke. Weet ek
sal gesond word.
Ons sal wees wat
God ons vra om te wees
heilig. God wil jou
gebruik want jyluister
na Sy stem.

My heart is hurting very much. I am so big –
I have turned 16 today. Do you know, Mommy,
I really appreciate everything you do for me?
You will receive wisdom to help me.
You must know I am going
to write a lot of books by myself.
You must know I am going to be healed.
We will be what God asks us to be – Holy.
God wants to use you because you listen to His voice.

In *A Message From God*, Aldo prophesied over his own life and said when he turned sixteen, his ministry would begin. At the writing of our second book, *Heaven & Hell*, he had already passed the milestone of his sixteenth birthday (as of April 2008).

'Has he started ministering yet?' everyone wants to know. I can only answer that God's ways are higher than our ways (see Isaiah 55:8-9). The hundreds of letters from all over the world, telling us how his testimony changed people's lives, was the beginning of his ministry.

When I think of one specific Sunday church service, I know God uses Aldo regardless of his outside condition. We were a bit late, and walked into a student-community church in Pretoria, while the worship was already in full swing. In his usual fashion, Aldo took to seeking God's countenance by lying face down and worshiping, without letting the curious stares bother him. Soon everybody around us became aware of his unrestrained adoration of God. Without having to say one word, the onlookers were brought to their knees, one by one, under the anointing of the Holy Spirit. Tears flowed freely, and hearts were changed.

Saint Francis of Assisi said: 'Preach the Gospel. And if necessary, use words.' I believe this is a good description of where Aldo is at in this season of his life. We all need to *live* the Gospel. The world needs to see Jesus in us, and not only hear us talk about Him.

After the service, a young man walked up to Tinus and said, 'Sir, I just want you to know – what I saw in your son today changed my life.' As Tinus and Aldo turned to leave, there was a whole crowd of students waiting to thank Aldo for his example of worshiping God. From this I understood that God only needs a willing vessel, not necessarily a perfect one; like Aldo wrote in his letter: *God wants to use you because you listen to His voice.*

> 'Then I went down to the potter's house,
> and there he was, making something at the wheel.
> And the vessel that he made of clay was marred in
> the hand of the potter;
> so he made it again into another vessel,
> as it seemed good to the potter to make.'
> *- Jeremiah 18:3-4 -*

want Jesus is oppad. God
se Jy wil my nou rеghe
maar Jy tyd is perfek.

Jesus is on His way. God says you want me to be perfectly healed now, but His time is perfect.

I always try to take my family with me when I speak at various events in our area. On one such occasion, the four of us were on our way to Bloemfontein for an open-air stadium rally. Holy Spirit clearly spoke to my heart while on the road: 'Retha, I want you to give Aldo an opportunity to speak after you have had your turn. He will know what to do.'

Doubtful, I replied, 'Lord, You know how his words always seem to come out different than the way he intends. Are You sure he is ready for this?'

Holy Spirit gently reassured me: 'Just trust Me.'

I shared my thoughts with Tinus, and to my surprise he immediately agreed. The big challenge was now to prepare Aldo for his first public appearance.

Before I went on stage, I pulled him aside to tell him of my intention. He stopped me in mid-sentence and said, 'It is OK with me, Mommy. Wisdom is with me,' and lifted his thumb into the air. I walked away with such peace in my heart, because I knew God had already prepared Aldo for what was to come.

After I finished preaching, I invited Aldo to come to the front. 'Aldo,' I said through the loudspeaker, 'will you please come closer? You don't have to come onto the stage, because I know the steps will be difficult to climb. You can stand in front of the stage, and say what is on your heart.'

Slowly he made his way to the front, walking without stumbling. He took his place in front of the stage, lifted both hands high into the air, and said: 'Jesus! Jesus! Jesus!'

Through the name above all names, the power of God was made manifest. People cried, stood up, and clapped loudly for the King of kings who is alive. Afterward, people came to thank us, and shared how Aldo touched their hearts. Many people accepted Jesus as their Lord and Savior that night.

There is a beautiful simplicity in the way the Holy Spirit comes and touches our hearts. When we minister from the overflow of our love relationship with God, our words (even if they are few) will be powerful. It is not who we are, how much money we have in the bank, or how well we can preach, but what kingdom we come from – *'for the Kingdom of God is not words, but power'* (see 1 Corinthians 4:20).

Aldo understands the power contained in Jesus' name. He knew nothing more had to be said. The key to walking in kingdom power is the anointing of the Holy Spirit. This anointing is very precious and will only be found in God's presence. Jesus, through His death on the cross, tore the veil that separated us from God. Now we can enter in with boldness, to come before His throne of grace to receive this anointing (see Hebrews 4:16).

God has enrolled Aldo and me in the school of His Spirit. For the past five years, Aldo and I have been attending this school with the Bible as our textbook, the Holy Spirit as our Teacher, and Jesus as our Perfect Example. Our goal is to hear the Father say: 'Thank you good and faithful servant,' on graduation day when Jesus comes to fetch us. As we grow and mature in the Spirit, the learning process becomes easier, even though the circumstances don't. For with every passed test, we learn to trust and love the Lord more.

To get to the next level of our schooling, we have to pass the test at the end of the lesson. These tests will only be passed through prayer, worship, and obeying the Word of God. The school of the Spirit is a practical school, where we often fall and get up, make mistakes and learn from them, trade in our ways for God's ways, and learn to trust God in all circumstances. Because Aldo and I also make many mistakes along the way, Psalms 37:23-24 has become our motto: *'The steps of a [good] man are directed and established by the Lord when He delights in his way.... Though he falls, he shall not be utterly cast down, for the Lord grasps his hand in support and upholds him.'* (AMP).

We can't afford to live and breathe and have our being in Christ only on Sunday mornings. To live in the Spirit is a '24/7' commitment. The Bible says: *'For **all** who are led by the Spirit of God are sons of God'* (Romans 8:14). Living in the Spirit is not only for the popular names we see on television, or exclusively for our pastor, or the heroes of the Bible, but for all the children of God! When Jesus tore the veil He gave all of us access to a life saturated with His presence.

The first lesson of the school of the Spirit is simple: *It all begins with Jesus!*

Jesus is the Way, the Truth, and the Life. He is the Gate by which we enter, to go to the Father. In Matthew 7:13-14 Jesus says: *'Enter by the narrow gate; for wide is the gate and broad is the way that leads to destruction, and there are many who go in by it. Because narrow is the gate and difficult is the way which leads to life, and there are few who find it.'*

To walk in the narrow way, we need to die to ourselves and be alive to Christ. Without dying to self, we will never experience the fullness of Christ. Many believers try to dodge the dying-to-self part of Christianity, and are only imitating the walk of faith. When I look back at my own life, and how I lived before our accident, I know it was void of power and anointing. I was a clanging cymbal and I lived a self-centered life where everything was only about me. How privileged I am that God gave me another chance to lay down my life, only to take it up again with Jesus!

Aldo's sixteenth birthday dawned with a quiet hush over the entire family. Secretly we all hoped he would be completely healed by now. According to my preconceived ideas, I thought God could only use him if he looked the way I wanted him to look. But God uses Aldo mightily for His Kingdom just the way he is. Truly, He uses the foolish things of this world to teach the wise!

> 'But God has chosen the foolish things
> of the world to put to shame the wise,
> and God has chosen the weak things of the world
> to put to shame the things which are mighty...'
> - 1 Corinthians 1:27 -

> *I saw myself preaching my first sermon.*
> *God says I already have what I need inside of me.*
> *People will just accept Jesus immediately.*
> *God has repeatedly told me, I already work for Him.*

If I had to sum up Jesus' earthly sermons, I would use the words *repentance* and *faith*. If these words and what they meant were so important to Him, we should also give much attention to the same areas in our Christian walk. That is why it is so important to repent of sin (especially unbelief), when the Holy Spirit convicts us. Repentance breaks down the walls the enemy tries to build between us and God.

Aldo is also just human, and like all of us, he daily needs to wash himself of the sin that so easily entangles. (Neither Aldo, nor I are 'super-holy' after our encounters with God – we battle with our sinful, human natures, like every other person who truly wants to follow Jesus. By His blood we are cleansed, and by His grace we are changed from glory to glory, but it is a daily process). Through repentance and prayer we allow God to cleanse us from sin, and fill us with His anointing.

I remember the one day, while I was busy in the kitchen, I heard Josh's voice floating through the window, 'Aldo, I don't want to play soccer with you anymore! You pray too much!' This is how it must be for all of us. We must continually be aware of God, in and around, us.

Aldo would very much like to have a special friend – more specifically, a girlfriend. The emphasis is on *friend*, because anything more than that belongs to his wife. We often explain to him that she is handpicked by God, and kept in a safe place especially for him, until the time is right. Usually our words bring comfort to his hurt, but some days he continues to ask when he will be ready to take a girl out for a milkshake.

According to the world's standard, boys and girls are allowed to be intimate with one another without limits. It doesn't matter anymore that they are not nearly mature enough to handle such serious relationships. I think there is a great need for pure friendship between boys and girls, where bodies are kept holy and hearts whole. Our heavenly Bridegroom wants our earthy marriages and relationships to reflect His holiness, so that those couples, whom He unites together, can start their lives with whole hearts, not broken pieces.

The one thing Aldo definitely doesn't lack is boldness. One day, he asked one of the new girls in school if she wanted to be his girlfriend. She wrote him a sweet letter in response: 'Aldo, God wants me to keep myself pure for my husband. But it would be wonderful to be your friend!' This letter is very special to Aldo.

To respond, Miss Patrys (our angel) came up with a brilliant idea. The next morning, he walked up to the girl and gave her a thumbs-up and a chocolate with the words *Friends Forever* on the wrapper. I praise God that this girl handled the situation so well and made my son feel special and wanted. It did wonders for his self-esteem!

When we walk in a shopping mall, he frequently asks us if we think thís or thát pretty girl is his wife. Once again, little Josh comes to our rescue, 'Aldo, you must focus on what God sent you back to do. You need to tell the world Jesus is alive. Don't get caught up in all this girlfriend nonsense!'

Inwardly, my heart smiles when I hear this, because I see how our whole family is walking this road with Aldo. Because Aldo does everything slower than other children his age, Tinus would sternly warn when his eyes linger, 'Aldo, you can look, but don't stare.'

As with the other obstacles, we have learned to laugh in the midst of difficult circumstances. Together, we are working through this hormone-adolescent phase, step-by-step, as a family. I know this is just one more area in which we can trust God for a breakthrough.

Somewhere, He is preparing a wife for Aldo after His own heart. Aldo frequently writes about her:

Wisdom shows me I will be married to a beautiful wife
that is going to love me very much.
He says He shows you how she is going to look.
God knows what my life will be like,
and my wife is going to go with me around the world.
Do you know there will be lots of girls who like me?
God says I cannot marry just any girl.
God says she will be very special.
I wish I could get to know her now already.
God lets everything work together for our good.
Thank You. Be patient...just be patient, Aldo.

I couldn't help but smile when I read his letter, because I can hear him preaching to himself!

I met a beautiful blond-haired girl, about Aldo's age, on a weekend camp I facilitated. Our testimony made quite an impression on her and she sent Aldo a letter with an accompanying photo.

Before he sat down to answer her letter, I saw him staring at her photo. Nervously, I wondered what he was going to write, because I could just imagine what his hormones were whispering in his ear.

Surprised, I read:

hallo Jana

Verseker was ek bare bly oor jou brief. Jy is bare mooi vrrng. Lyk ek regtig mooi vir jou. Lewe is bare kosbaar en sy moet asb by ons kom kuier. Jesus sal jou boetie gesond maak

Jy moet net bly glo. Wees gereed want Jesus is oppad ek was in die hemel. hou jou rein Jy is spesiaal vir Jesus

Lief ac Alto.

> *Hello, Jana.*
> *I was very happy because of your letter!*
> *You are beautiful to me.*
> *Do I really look beautiful to you, too?*
> *Life is precious, and you should please come and visit me.*
> *Jesus will heal your brother. You must just keep on believing.*
> *Be ready, because Jesus is on His way. I was in heaven.*
> *Keep yourself pure. You are special to Jesus.*
> *Love, Aldo*

This is the life of my seventeen-year-old son. Being a teenager is difficult for him, too. He goes through growing pains like all the rest, and as a family, we go through it with him. He gets frustrated when we don't give him enough space to be independent. Like other households, we have normal parent/teenager fights. Tinus is very strict, but Aldo loves and respects his father. Every once in a while, Aldo will give his 'frustration yell' just to let all of us know we have to respect his opinion. Soon afterwards, he will write:

> *Mommy, I am sorry I yelled. Will you please still love me?*
> *My morning was hectic, but I don't want to be this way.*
> *God will take out everything that is ugly in me.*

For sure, I will love you, Aldo – unconditionally!
Because that is how Jesus loves me.
He loves the imperfect...*perfectly.*

The reality of
the Kingdom of God

Jy was in die troonkamer
wys my as b wat jy so bare
laat huil want Jesus
het jou so styf vasgehou
my werk is om vir mense
te bid want jy het
my geoffer aan God.
mamma weet nog nie
want mamma kyk vas,
? sy werk doen.
wat jy sien. gaan jy
jou groot wonder nog
beleef ek sal gesond
wees.

> *You were in the throne room.*
> *Please show me what made you cry like that,*
> *because I saw Jesus holding you very tightly.*
> *My assignment is to pray for people*
> *because you sacrificed me to God.*
> *You don't know yet,*
> *because you only focus on what you can see.*
> *You will experience a great miracle – I will be healed.*

When Aldo started writing messages about the throne room, I was totally baffled. On more than one occasion he described in detail what I thought only God and I knew – private moments of intimacy between the King and me.

There was a time when Aldo was extremely sick. We struggled with his epilepsy and as our spiritual battle dragged on, I slowly but surely became discouraged. I started doubting whether I had heard God correctly in the first place. Negative thoughts plagued me, and I asked Jesus if He was really going to heal and restore Aldo completely.

The first prize of my faith would be for Aldo's body *and* soul *and* spirit to be in line with God's Word. Aldo's healing can't be at the expense of His calling. I want my child to live in line with God's Word in all areas of his life. If not, I would rather walk this difficult road, while God is busy molding him into the man He wants him to be.

Without telling him about these doubts milling through my heart, Aldo wrote one morning:

> *Jesus says that what you asked Him last night will definitely happen. Why do you doubt, Mommy?*

On one of my trips to Indonesia, I had a clear vision of where God would be taking me and my family. While ministering at an event, the crowd spontaneously started calling on the name of Jesus. Over and over, the only word everyone said was, 'Jesus! Jesus! Jesus!' The anointing resting upon us was so strong! It felt tangible as hundreds of voices called in unity. The glory of God was there, and just as the Prophet Ezekiel describes in Ezekiel 3:23, the people fell to their faces in His presence.

> 'So I arose and went out into the plain, and behold, the glory of the LORD stood there, like the glory which I saw by the River Chebar, and I fell on my face.'
> - *Ezekiel 3:23* -

I too, couldn't stand under such a heavy anointing. There, flat on my face, I had an open-heaven experience and I could see the holy host of angels all around us. In my spirit, I could sense God picking me up ever so gently and putting me on His lap. His love was overwhelming, and He said, 'I want to teach you, Retha. To do the impossible, you have to see the invisible. Come; let Me show you what I see.'

I then saw my family with me on stage, and we were standing before a very large crowd. Aldo was standing with a microphone in his hand, evangelizing and preaching to the people. Josh and Tinus were also there with us. The Spirit of God was hovering like a cloud over the meeting, and people were delivered, healed, and even the dead were raised.

When I eventually got up from the ground, I could see the people around me were having their own intimate meetings with God. They were crying or laughing, some were still lying on the ground engulfed by the wave of His presence, and others were worshiping with arms held high.

A young Indonesian lady ran toward me and kept on shouting, 'Did you see Him? Did you see Him? Jesus stood right in front of me and asked me why I never believed that He was alive before.' She told me of all the people who tried to lead her to Christ in the past. She never wanted to believe them, because she was brought up in another faith. That is the power of the revealed Christ – one second in God's presence and your life will never be the same again.

When I finally arrived home after two weeks of a busy schedule, Aldo wrote:

> *I saw Jesus showed you what is going to happen one day. Do you believe now, Mommy?*

How can it be that Aldo knows things only God and I know?

> *Live like God wants you to. Please show the world God's love.*

> *Go with God to heaven, because who will tell of what I saw there? God allows it; please go to heaven, because God wants you to understand where I was. Please tell the world what God shows me.*

In my search to understand more about this mystery, I decided to purposefully listen to Aldo as he walks through the house and prays.

'Wisdom,' he addresses the Holy Spirit, 'please, open the heavens for me.'

I pause a moment to think about his prayer. 'What exactly is an open heaven?' I wonder to myself. And once again I realize there is so much more that I have to learn. I so desperately want the fullness of God, and to have that, I need to walk in the Spirit with Him – that means: heaven needs to meet earth. Just as with Jacob, I believe there is a ladder whereby angels climb up and down, but we will only experience this if we walk in the Spirit (see Genesis 28:12).

What I *do* know, is the more I repent and deal with the sin in my life, the purer my fellowship with Jesus becomes, and the easier it is to take His hand and walk with Him in this open-heaven reality.

wie mag opgaan na die Heilige berg hy wat ryn vuh hart is

> *Who may ascend the holy hill? He who has a pure heart.*

> 'Who may ascend into the hill of the LORD? Or who may stand in His holy place? He who has clean hands and a pure heart, who has not lifted up his soul to an idol, nor sworn deceitfully.'
> *- Psalm 24:3-4 -*

To stay clean, we need to continually wash ourselves. Just as a person needs to shower every day to keep their body clean and fresh, so our spirit and soul need to be kept clean by repentance and then forgiveness through the blood of the Lamb. When we study the Word of God, Holy Spirit will use it as a mirror to show us where we need to wash. If He convicts us of sin, we must not fight Him. Rather, we must humble ourselves under His hand, repent, and turn away from our sin, toward God.

'Therefore, submit to God.
Resist the devil and he will flee from you.
Draw near to God and He will draw near to you.
Cleanse your hands, you sinners;
and purify your heart, you double-minded.'
- James 4:7-8 -

The more I meditate on what an open heaven really is, the clearer Jesus' words become: *Let Thy Kingdom come, as it is in heaven, here on earth also* (see Matthew 6:10). We need to understand that *Thy Kingdom—His Kingdom—*and the laws governing it, in order to see heaven and earth meet and become one.

His Kingdom is God's sovereignty overflowing in our daily lives. The outward manifestation will be signs, miracles, and wonders. God has destined each of His children to walk with authority as kings and priests in His Kingdom (see Revelation 5:10). The precondition for this authority is a life fully surrendered to the Lord. You have to lay down your life, pick up your cross, and follow Jesus only.

'Then Jesus said to His disciples,
"If anyone desires to come after Me, let him deny himself,
and take up his cross, and follow Me.
For whoever desires to save his life will lose it,
but whoever loses his life for My sake will find it.'
- Matthew 16:24-25 -

The person who chooses to trade the temporary gratification of following fleshly desires for the truth of the Word of God, will receive the Kingdom and the abundant life Jesus speaks of in John 10:10. This is why Aldo knows so much about the fullness of God, because he has died to himself. Nothing of this world impresses him anymore.

> *Jesus says I want to make you happy again, and*
> *God says that He wants to reveal Himself to you again.*
> *God says that you and I want to please Him.*
> *Did you see me and Jesus last night?*
> *There was an angel with Him. I want to go to heaven again.*
> *Did you know Jesus stood here next to your bed*
> *and blessed you? He wants you to trust Him with the contract.*
> *You want wisdom. God gives us His grace, and know*
> *that I am going to be like God said I would be.*
> *How will others live without the help of God?*
> *I say the wrong words when I speak.*
> *Please, Mommy, will you help me?*

We will always receive firsthand revelation in His presence. These are the real treasures of life. We don't need head knowledge, but heart knowledge (revelation knowledge). Just like precious stones or diamonds, they are hidden very deep and will only be found by those who persistently seek. We will not find these treasures through superficial works, but in intimacy with the King. Superficial works and pretenses keep us busy and distracted on the surface, while Jesus wants us to go deeper. Jesus said it so accurately to Peter when they struggled fruitlessly all night to catch some fish: 'Peter, you need to throw your nets in deeper. I know you have been out on the sea all night, but throw deeper!' (see Luke 5:4-6).

By 'works' I don't mean those acts of obedience when we serve, love, and give in accordance to the leading of the Holy Spirit. This 'laying down of our lives,' and obedience, is very important to God and these works will be a testimony of our faith and our love for the Lord. The Bible clearly says:

> 'And I saw the dead, small and great,
> standing before God, and books were opened.
>
> And another book was opened, which is the Book of Life.
> And the dead were judged according to their works,
> by the things which were written in the books.'
> - *Revelation 20:12* -

By 'works' I mean the masks we wear, trying to impress God or man through the flesh. I see a lot of people who think their relationship with God is at a good place because they are good citizens and they do kind acts every now and again. I would know – I was one of them. *Charity* and I were best friends. But remember, even though we bestow all our goods to feed the poor, but have not love, it profits us nothing (see 1 Corinthians 13:3).

I can tell you from experience, one moment in His presence will change your life forever. That is where spirit connects to Spirit. With everything in me I seek this intimate *agape*-love relationship with God (*agape* is the Greek word that indicates the highest form of love). Only His love for me brings real purpose to my life.

Let me explain by describing another one of these heavenly throne room experiences I had in 2008. One night, as I lay down on my bed before falling asleep, I was aware of how I suddenly felt as light as air. I could feel how God was picking me up and taking me higher and higher. I was suddenly in the midst of a room, filled with a blinding white light. I intrinsically knew the light was different from the earthly light I was accustomed to. On earth, if we want sunlight to brighten up a room, we have to open the curtains and allow the light to flood the room from the outside in. However, this light was most definitely shining from the inside out.

The closer I drew to the Source of light, the more I became aware of humility, compassion, mercy, love...until the weight of God's character engulfed me. It was *holiness* flowing like electricity through my body. All I wanted to do was to fall down on my face before God, repent of my sin, and cry, 'Holy, holy, holy is the Lord God Almighty!'

His presence is pure love and His love is unconditional. There are no words to fully describe His awesome presence. Everything else seems dull and grey in comparison. Deep inside of me, I knew this is what God created me for – to be *one* with Him.

'Yes, My dear child, this is My desire for all My children. To live in the reality of My kingdom can only be achieved if you are one with Me. My thoughts, My words, My actions... *through you.*'

The Holy Spirit handed me a cloak of humility. It is a very special cloak, soft and beautiful, and it fits me like a glove. The reason the Holy Spirit only handed me the cloak now, is because I could never fit into it before. My pride and self-righteousness puffed me up, and the cloak would have been too small. I remembered First Peter 5:5: '...*Clothe yourselves, all of you, with humility... For God sets Himself against the proud...but gives grace...to the humble.*'

Before the vision ended, God showed me a Bible and gave me a message for His people, 'Retha, go and tell My children they will be judged according to My Word.'

Even though I was standing in front of the throne of grace, I felt a holy fear when I heard these words and I knew we needed to take heed of the warning.

I also knew I wasn't the only one before the throne of grace; and that there were countless others gathered with me seeking God's countenance. God is raising up an army of warriors who seek Him with pure hearts and worship Him in spirit and truth.

Jesus se ons is Sy warriors
en ons sal god se woord
verkondig oor die wêreld.
Wie sal gaan waar Jesus
ons stuur. God sê ons
sal Sy stem hoor en weet
om te doen. Weet namma
dat god weet wat jou
begeerte is van hart.

Jesus says we are His warriors and
we will preach God's Word over the world.
Who will go where Jesus sends them?
God says we will hear His voice and know what to do.
Mommy, God says He knows what the desire of your heart is.

My question to you is this: *'Are you a part of this army?'*

The invitation to be a warrior for Jesus is not just for Aldo and me. It is for you, too!

The Holy Spirit is the One who shows us the way into God's Kingdom and teaches us to live daily in His Kingdom reality. He is also the One who prepares us, and equips us for this spiritual battle.

'But when He, the Spirit of Truth…comes,
He will guide you into all the Truth….
For He will not speak His own message…
but He will tell whatever He hears…and
He will announce and declare…things that are to come….'
- *John 16:33 AMP* -

All of God's children received the seal of the Holy Spirit when they opened their hearts, and invited Jesus to come in; but the infilling and overflow of the Holy Spirit comes when we diligently seek it out (see 2 Corinthians 1:22 and Luke 11:9-13). Like the five wise virgins, we need to buy the precious oil for our lamps and not be found with empty lamps and smoldering wicks when Jesus returns (see Matthew 25:1-13).

Without the anointing of the Holy Spirit, we can try to minister with our God-given gifts, but we will only end up striving. The Spirit brings the power of God. The single candle will become a blazing fire, when anointed with His most precious oil.

Once we have tasted the love, grace, compassion, and sweetness of God's passion, our appetite for worldly things will be ruined forever. That is God's plan for His Bride from Genesis to Revelation – to taste and see that God is good, for it is the *goodness* of God that leads people to repentance (see Psalm 34:8; Romans 2:4).

God said to me, 'Retha, you will never minister about anything that you have not tasted.'

That is why I can keep on standing, throughout all my trials; because I know God is going to use these trails to help someone else later on. Throughout every trial I can hear God inviting me into His secret place, 'Come, Retha. Come and drink from My living waters – you will never thirst again. Here, in My presence, you are safe from the storm. You are protected by My love. I have prepared a table for you in the face of your enemies. Eat of My manna – eat My Word. Taste and see that I am good.'

Aldo saw me there in front of the throne of grace and he wrote:

> *Did you see God like I saw Him, Mommy?*
> *God sat on His throne and told me I must tell the world*
> *Jesus is alive. He promised me I will be healed and*

Flesh will not 'see' God. Aldo is describing seeing His glory; the weighty presence of the Lord. There, in the Holy of Holies, face down before His throne, I could only weep because of His love and the privilege to be a child of God. Just like Moses, I want to spend as much time as I can in front of His throne so that His glory will also reflect on my face. It is my desire to be completely one with Him, so that I won't even have to say a word, but His presence that I carry in me (the Lion of Judah living inside of me), will manifest in signs, wonders, and miracles in the world around me. It will be His works flowing through me as I walk in obedience.

For so many years I missed out on this, because I was distracted by tradition, comfort, trying to fit in, and fear of what I didn't understand. God wants all His children to walk in the fullness of His Kingdom.

Visions, dreams and heavenly experiences are part of our inheritance in the Kingdom, because if we are one with Him, it will be to the glory of His name.

> 'And it shall come to pass afterward that
> I will pour out My Spirit on all flesh;
> your sons and your daughters shall prophesy,
> your old men shall dream dreams,
> your young men shall see visions.
> And also on My menservants and on My maidservants
> I will pour out My Spirit in those days.'
> *- Joel 2:28-29 -*

Wil mamma weer god
se troonkamer ingaan.

ek gaan elke oggend weer in. Wil mamma wys wont daar is iemand wat jou ken

Do you want to go into God's throne room again, Mommy? I go in every day. There is someone that you know there.

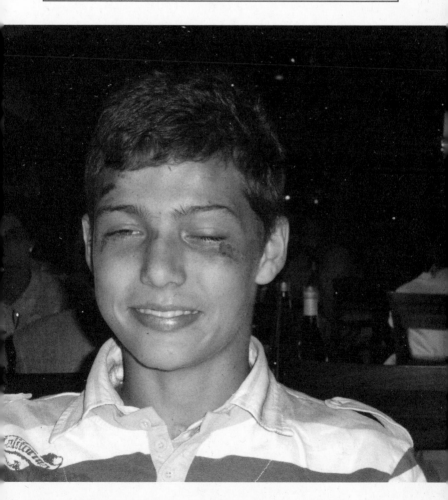

Pure water
for a thirsty soul

Nou vandag gaan ek, sal ek
wees wat Jesus wil hê
ek moet wees. Ek moet
'n profeet wees wat
mense waarsku dat
Jesus kom ons kom
haal. Saam water
en aardbewings sal
ons die ~~Fie~~ god se ~~krag~~
en mag beleef wat ons
dien Sal jy gaan en die
mense waarske dat daar
water kom Ek gaan word
soos Mosus wat die mense
gewaarsku het
dat God
berg sou kom

From today I will be what Jesus wants me to be.
I have to be a prophet that warns people Jesus is on
His way to fetch us. Through water and earthquakes
we will experience God's strength and might.
Will you go and warn the people that there is water coming?
I will become like Moses that warned the people
that God will be coming to the mountain.

We have learned to listen when Aldo prophesies through his letters. We didn't always. In the beginning, all of these things were very new and daunting to us. People are usually afraid of the unknown, and we were no exception.

The first time one of his prophecies came to pass, was about six months after the accident. At that time, he was still in the wheelchair, head drooping, left eye blind, and worst of all, silent. The accident was in June 2004, and in December of that year (while we were on holiday) he wrote letters, warning me that he saw a lot of water coming and people hanging from palm trees. Here are excerpts of some of his letters:

Will you go and find out when water can hit us as a river? We will see a lot of water, also earthquakes.

Will you go and warn the people, Mommy? Also, go and tell God that you will be obedient. God showed me.

Mommy, you must rest. You will go there.

I see a lot of water coming; only the palm trees are left standing and people are hanging from the trees. It will be after the "Day of Reconciliation."
(The Day of Reconciliation is a South African holiday commemorated on the 16th of December.)

Like I said, this was very new to us. Tinus and I initially thought the medication was too strong. I couldn't wait to get back home to our doctor and get a prescription for a lower dosage.

A few days later, the news reports started streaming in about the tsunami that hit the greater Asia area. I was still Mrs. South Africa at that time, and the organizers of the pageant asked me if I would be willing to go and help as a relief worker in Indonesia.

The moment I stepped off the airplane in Banda Aceh, I saw what Aldo described in one of his letters. Only the palm trees were left standing – literally. The implications of what I saw rippled through my mind, and I could no longer deny that my twelve-year-old son, sitting in a wheelchair at home, was an instrument of God.

This was the first prophecy that came to pass: the tsunami that hit the coastland of Indonesia on December 26, 2004.

After this initial prophecy, there have been many others about various topics. Now, he frequently prophesies about world events and especially the future of Israel.

He wrote one day:

> *Ma'am, read Ezekiel 36.*
> *Jesus shows me it is the oil in Israel, what it is all about.*

I read his letter and said, 'Yes, whatever, Aldo. What would you know about the war in Israel?' He looked at me with his one eye and said, 'Ma'am, you will repent of these words!' (He always calls me "Ma'am" and Tinus, "Mister," when he prophesies.)

al die olie is in Israel. god
se weet ek waar ja ek weet
hy het my gaan wys wysheid
wys my waar ek sien die

> *All the oil is in Israel. God asks: do I know where? Yes, I know.*
> *He showed me. Wisdom showed me where.*

> *Ma'am, do you know He said what is happening now in Israel will lead to Armageddon? Please, Ma'am. Believe me when I say Jesus is on His way. He knows you know. Wisdom says I will be healed quickly. He says I know where He is sending me. Listen to God. He says work, because He is on His way.*

> *Do you know God gave me wisdom of where all the oil*
> *is in Israel? Think about it. Do you want to know*
> *what Moses told me in my house in heaven?*
> *Wisdom, my God, shows me where all the oil is in Israel.*

Aldo has a special love for Moses (maybe because he identifies so closely with him – Moses also struggled to talk). One day Tinus tried to encourage him once again to speak a bit faster, 'Come now, Aldo. Mommy and I also want a turn to talk.' Aldo looked him straight in the eye and said, 'Don't stress, Dad. Moses told me he couldn't speak fast, too.' Who can argue with a comment like that!

Aldo wrote a lot about America, their financial system, and the Presidential election, at the time when America's financial problems started making headline news.

> *People will invite you to America. You must go.*
> *You are Jesus' hands and feet. Please give a word*
> *to America that I will give you.*
> *Their Minister must hear it.*
> *I was there.*

The only way he could have been 'there' is if God took him there in a vision while he was asleep; because believe me, his body was safe and sound in his bed every night. Later, I was invited to America, and gave the following message in an American church:

> *Please show people what Jesus says of America.*
> *For those who don't accept Him and make Him King,*
> *He will take His hand off them.*
> *Israel must be supported.*
> *God says to go to His country that others reject.*
> *You will see – America's currency will drop,*
> *and Israel is what it is about.*

These are very serious words, and from experience we have learned not to take them lightly. But the children of God need not fear anything, but only worshipfully fear God Himself. Psalm 91 reassures us:

> 'He who dwells in the secret place of the Most High
> shall abide under the shadow of the Almighty...'
>
> 'Because you have made the LORD, who is my refuge,
> even the Most High, your dwelling place,
> No evil shall befall you, nor shall any plague
> come near your dwelling;
> For He shall give His angels charge over you,
> to keep you in all your ways.'
> *- Psalm 91:1,9-11 -*

Jesus se aan die wat hom dien sal hy bonatuurlik seen.

Jesus says those who serve Him, He will bless supernaturally.

Aldo not only prophecies over world events, but he also speaks prophetically into our personal lives, our family, and the ministry. Often when I stand before a difficult decision, he will encourage me through his letters and give me an indication of the right direction.

The following letter was as a result of a big financial decision I had to make:

*Jesus says you showed Him money is not
what is important to you. God says He sees your heart.
I will be wise like Solomon. Be prepared.
He shows me how I stand and prophecy
in front of thousands of people.*

For the most part, Aldo was extremely sick throughout 2008. But regardless of all these struggles, he would still pick up his pen and prophesy as the Holy Spirit led.

The Lord usually talks to me in pictures, and He gave me this vision to describe Aldo and his letters: He showed me a ramshackle water-well. The part of the well that is visible to the human eye is broken and seems beyond repair, but there is a treasure hidden beyond what the eye can see. Deep within the well, there is pure, living, water.

Holy Spirit spoke to my heart: 'In the same way, there is pure water hidden in Aldo's spirit, Retha. Don't get distracted or discouraged by what you can see with your eyes. When he writes, the bucket is lowered and a sweet stream of living water is brought forth.'

Please know I appreciate you so much.
My heart hurts when I disappoint you,
and I wish I could make you happy again.
God says I know I will be a prophet. I am truly a prophet.
I love you, Mommy. Do you know, Mommy?
Wisdom shows me how I lay my hands on people,
and they realize God is alive because they will
be perfectly healed. Did I hurt you again?
God says, know for certain that
what He has started He will finish.

For the most part, all the outside world can see is the broken parts of the well (Aldo's body), because in our day-to-day life we battle with the symptoms of the brain injury. The water that comes from the well (the truth flowing from his spirit when he writes), is our gift from God. It keeps us humble and gives us hope. Through these letters, God constantly reminds us that Aldo should be treated as a normal boy. Even if he seems different to the natural eye, we know there is a treasure hidden deep within him.

> *Jesus shows me what I am going to do is prophesy.*
> *He must be your first love.*

Any prophets' words must be tested and proven true; and I look very closely at Aldo's prophecies to measure them against the Word of God. Furthermore, a tree will be known by its fruit. If the fruit is good, the whole tree is good. I believe, anyone seeking to walk with the Lord in spirit and truth (being anchored in Jesus Christ and led by the Holy Spirit), will be able to hear and convey His words. All He is asking for is obedience and faith.

I would rather drink pure water from a broken well, than drink dirty water from a well that is only beautiful to look at. Without the pure water, the well is only a religious structure – beautiful to look at, but lacking life-giving power. Only faith in God gives true life.

A sip of pure water will sustain me through another day in the desert while I am waiting for my promise to be fulfilled, because I know the price Jesus paid for me to drink it. Jesus said: *'Whoever drinks of the water that I shall give him will never thirst. But the water that I shall give him will become in him a fountain of water springing up into everlasting life'* (John 4:14).

> *He shows me I will lay my hands on people*
> *that are dying and then they will live.*
> *My job is to pray for people.*
> *Jesus wants to exalt God.*
> *Do you want to know what God says?*
> *He says you and I will minister together.*
> *Did you feel His power right now?*

> 'How wonderful it is to know we possess
> this precious treasure in earthen vessels,
> that the excellence of the power may be of God and not of us.'
> *- See 2 Corinthians 4:7 -*

It is the power of the Living God that keeps me standing. This road we are walking on is so difficult some days, but the anointing and strength that keeps us going is totally supernatural – and I choose it above all else!

Yes, above everything.

I choose Aldo the way he looks like at the moment and serving God with everything in him, above a completely healed body that is sold out to the world. I have told this to God many times.

Retha in Banda Aceh after the tsunami, December 2004

To do the impossible,
you need to see the invisible

Jesus was by my gister
nag hy se ons moet
net bly glo ek sal
genees. Wees het
geduldig jy sal sien
ek sal wees wat god
gese het

Jesus se jy was
by hom en toe
ays hy vir jou ek
het n aanval. Mamma
wil weer gaan en Jesus
se elke hag hou
Jy sal alles sien
wat ek sien Wil
weer hemel toe gaan
Leer mense wat god
se hy is lief vir almal
en hy soek ons lewers.

> *Jesus was with me last night.*
> *He says we only have to keep on believing I will be healed.*
> *Just be patient – you will see I will become*
> *what God said I will be. Jesus says you were with Him,*
> *and there He showed you I was going to have*
> *another (epileptic) attack. Mommy, you want to go*
> *(to the throne room) again and Jesus says He*
> *will take you there every night.*
> *You will see everything I see. I want to go to heaven again.*
> *Teach people what God says –*
> *He says He loves everybody and He wants our lives.*

In June 2008, Tinus and I went on a trip to Israel with friends. We drove from Egypt to Eilat, through the Sinai desert, in a small taxi bus without air-conditioning. Just a few grueling hours in the desert sun gave me new respect for the Israelites who endured this harsh weather for forty years! In vain, I kept on looking into the sky for any sign of the cloud that gave protection to God's chosen people on their journey. Now I know, without a doubt, that without God's cloud of grace, they would have been toast!

The reason we had to endure the desert was to get to the starting point of our tour: Eilat, and the wonders of the Red Sea. Everyone was eager to take hold of their long-awaited prize and dive right into the cool waters with their snorkeling gear – everyone, except Retha. I had never snorkeled before, and being a real farm girl, I admit to being afraid of this new experience. I didn't really want to go into the water. All the equipment scared me, and I felt much safer in my comfort zone on the beach.

After Tinus convinced me to go in, I put on all the gear, but kept standing on the beach. Holy Spirit then started speaking to my heart: 'Retha, you have all the gear on, but you still can't see anything because you are only standing on the beach. Just like this, there are a lot of people in church who call themselves believers, because they have the right gear on, but they don't live what they preach. They have a form of godliness, but deny its power' (see 2 Timothy 3:5).

I decided to face my fear and walk toward the water. That is all it took – one definitive decision. Tinus took my hand and helped me into the water. My husband is a wonderfully, patient teacher. He told me what to expect and what to avoid. Ever so gently he coached me into the water.

My first attempt wasn't very successful. I put my head into the water, and from pure anxiety I took a nervous gasp through the snorkel. The next moment, the water overwhelmed me. I pulled up and immediately tried to make for dry land. 'No, no. This is too difficult for me. I am a farm girl. Snorkeling is not for me!'

As I scurried out of the water, Holy Spirit stopped me in my tracks and said, 'Relax, Retha. You are always the one saying you have strength for all things through Christ Jesus. Tell Me, what do you see?'

I took a long look to the left and then to the right and answered, 'Lord, I can only see the desert stretching out to my left and the endless ocean to my right.'

Again He said to my heart, 'What you say is correct, and that is exactly where most of My children's vision is held captive. They either complain about the barrenness of the desert, or stand paralyzed by the fear of the deep ocean. Murmuring and fear keep My people in bondage. Take a step of faith, put your head under the water, relax, and behold My beauty.'

After I put my head in the water for the second time, I stood in awe. What I saw completely took my breath away. I saw a whole new world. A world I never could have imagined. I saw fish of all the colors of the rainbow, in every shape and size. There was no noise in this new reality – only peace. I saw the unseen. Only through Jesus' eyes will we see what lies beyond the veil.

After a long time of playing in God's swimming pool and enjoying the beauty of His creation, I got out and went to sit by myself on the beach, with tears streaking down my cheeks. I had no words to explain the greatness of God I had just experienced.

What I had been preaching for so long, God made tangible: *we first need to see the invisible, to do the impossible*. While I was standing in the water, too stubborn and too afraid to take a step of faith into the unknown, I was held bound by what my eyes could see. The dry desert and the depths of the ocean spoke of discontentment and fear. As long as my focus was on what I *could see*, I was oblivious to the treasures right under my nose that I *couldn't see*. We need to ask God to open our spiritual eyes to see beyond the natural. In the unseen we will find the fulfillment of God's promises.

'Retha, I just taught you about faith,' Holy Spirit said. 'You first had to trust Me, and look through My eyes, before you could see the other life – far above what you could hope or pray! The road is lonely, but all My treasures are hidden there. It is no use if you have all the equipment, but you don't use it. If you don't take a step of faith, you will never be able to see through My eyes.'

There were so many times in the past that the Holy Spirit instructed me: 'Tell My people that they can have what they say, but they say what they have.' So now I ask, what do our words reflect? Do they reflect what we see in our natural circumstances, or the potential of what God can do with these circumstances? Are we murmuring and complaining, full of doubt and fear; or are we standing on God's Word, trusting Him for our breakthrough? One step of faith toward God can open up a world so rich in treasure, that it will be far greater than anything we could ever have thought possible (see Ephesians 3:20).

This practical lesson of walking by faith and not by sight

came just at the right time. When we came home, we returned to a very sick child.

Roughly two years after the accident, Aldo started suffering from epileptic seizures. According to the doctors, these types of epileptic attacks are common to patients with his degree of head injuries. They were usually mild attacks, but soon after our return from Israel, his epileptic seizures increased in ferocity and frequency. These attacks would now occur as much as three times in one night, and would leave Aldo depleted of strength for the next few days following the attack. It badly influenced his balance, his concentration, and left him confused and bewildered.

Not only Aldo, but also the entire family experienced the trauma of these attacks. We did everything we could possibly do. We made sure he ate according to his special diet and took his pills exactly as the doctor prescribed. We prayed and fasted, but still the attacks came. These epileptic attacks drained my strength just as they did Aldo's. I later felt so discouraged that I would just remain quiet for days on end, not saying much, only seeking God's mercy and grace on my knees.

While driving home one day, I asked God this question, 'Lord, how do I receive this life of victory, a life in abundance, that I so desperately seek?'

Holy Spirit reminded me of this Scripture in response: *'I have been crucified with Christ; it is no longer I who live, but Christ lives in me; and the life which I now live in the flesh I live by faith in the Son of God, who loved me and gave Himself for me'* (Galatians 2:20).

I realized it was God's way of telling me He doesn't want to improve the old 'self,' just so we will be a new improved version of the old man. Rather, He wants to crucify the old man, so we can be resurrected to a new life as a new creation. *Victory* comes when we release our grip on our life and hand it to Jesus to do with it as He pleases, regardless of what the outcome might be.

In my spirit I heard God say, 'Retha, don't look at your weakness as failure. Know that in your weakness; My strength is made perfect (see 2 Corinthians 12:9). You need to stand firm in your faith, not forgetting what I told you in the throne room. You have a promise that Aldo will be healed and that he will tell the world that Jesus is alive. Hold on to that promise.' (I can confess that I hold on to this wonderful promise with everything in me!)

'Faith is not asking the same things of Me over and over again, thinking I didn't hear you the first time. Faith is to say "thank You," while believing My promises, and enduring until the end. If you believe My promises, you have grown in maturity, and you show that you understand My character. In order to see the unseen, you need to believe My Word. Retha, I act on faith, not on need. Make sure you have sowed your seed of faith, for it is written, *faith is the substance of things hoped for and the evidence of things not seen* (see Hebrews 11:1). While the seed is still under the ground, no one can see it; but with time a great harvest will come in.'

The height of our struggle with the epilepsy was in June 2008, just after Tinus and I returned from Israel. After our trip, I wanted to spend some quality time with my children and took them down to Cape Town for the school holidays. Tinus had to stay in Hartebeespoort for the week to finish up some projects at work, but would catch up with us over the weekend.

On the second night the children and I were alone at the beach house, Aldo had a series of epileptic attacks (the worst I had ever seen). The best I could do was to try and hold his body down during the convulsions. The first attack was extremely intense. As the foam came out of his mouth and his face turned blue, I went cold right to the core of my being. I thought my son was going to die, and the only thing I could think of was to shout the name of Jesus. I kept on calling over and over, 'Jesus! Jesus! Jesus!'

After what felt like an eternity, his body finally calmed

down and the color returned to his face as he started to breathe normally.

Numbed by the shock, I put him to bed again and sat quietly for a long time at the end of the bed. After a while, I climbed in next to him and Josh in our big bed, to try and get some rest. A little while later, I awoke to the sound of Josh screaming, 'Aldo is having another attack, Mommy!' We faced the next onslaught within a few hours from the first.

'Don't worry, Joshie. Jesus is here with us, and He won't let anything happen to Aldo!' I said through my tears. As the seizure subsided and his body quieted down, I sat with my head in my hands on the corner of our bed not knowing what to do. Should I call for an ambulance? Should I just stand in faith and pray? Should I phone Tinus?

I put Aldo to bed once again. His breathing returned to normal, and I slowly started to relax, but sleep was out of the question now. My tears flowed freely, and the sound of the waves outside, crashing against the rocks, so accurately described the feelings in my heart. I felt storm-tossed, lonely, and lost.

An hour or two passed and then the next attack wave hit. This time I yelled loudly, 'No, Jesus, no! This can't be happening again! You need to help us, Jesus!' By this time I felt so weak I couldn't even pray. The tears that hadn't stopped flowing, now dripped on Aldo's blue face. As the final storm subsided, I didn't even bother to put him to bed again. I held him tightly and just said, 'Jesus, Jesus, Jesus,' all night long as I rocked him to sleep.

Aldo was floored for the next few days following the attack. After he recovered somewhat, he wrote:

> *Mommy, I was scared I was going to die*
> *the other night when you held my body so tightly.*
> *Did you see the angels that were around us?*
> *Jesus took me to God in that time. God said it is not*
> *my time to die. I still have too much work to do.*

I have seen angels in the past, but why couldn't I see the angels around us when I needed them the most?

Holy Spirit answered, 'Retha, you couldn't see the angels through all your tears. You were trying to look for them with your flesh eyes. This road you are walking on is the road of the cross. The moment you bend your knee before Me, I drape the cloak of humility over you, and intimacy follows. Your battles will be fought and won on your knees.'

> *I love You Jesus. Thank You that You were with me*
> *when I was sick last night. You held me tightly*
> *and You showed me that I will be healed.*
> *Please show my Mom and Dad*
> *that they shouldn't be afraid when I get sick.*
> *You are definitely alive and You want us to*
> *trust You with my healing. Like Moses,*
> *I will go and show the world what God's glory looks like.*
> *Mommy, will you trust Jesus with everything you have?*
> *You and I are going to preach God's Word one day.*

The day after these epileptic attacks, my phone rang nonstop from people seeking spiritual counseling, or a shoulder to cry on. They had no idea of the difficult night I had just endured. On the inside, my heart was completely broken and I felt I was the one that needed an encouraging word, not the other way around.

'My son just broke up with his girlfriend. Please pray with me, I am in a total state!' one mother said to me. There I realized once again how quickly we get wrapped up in our own problems, losing sight of what is really important. We should scale our problems from one to ten – ten being death – and reconsider if we should complain or rather jump up and down because of our amazing life. People make a habit of complaining, instead of counting their blessings and being thankful for God's great grace.

A few days later we were still on holiday, but under "house arrest" because Aldo was so sick. One afternoon, Aldo and I were just lying on the bed when he had his next attack. This time I struggled even more to control my wild emotions. I raised my voice and almost yelled, 'Jesus, where are You? What do You want me to do, Lord? I can't do this by myself!'

'Not by might, not by power, but by My Spirit,' says the Lord God Almighty. *'Worship Me through all the pain, Retha. That is the last key to victory.'*

The moment I started singing, things changed. I was no longer afraid or anxious or angry. I took Aldo in my arms and sang songs of praise to my God over him. It felt like I was watching a movie, seeing Aldo and myself playing the lead roles. Gone was all the turmoil of the previous attacks. The situation was no different, but something inside me changed. This time everything looked different and I was living in this new reality: *It is no longer I that live, but Christ in me!*

'My brethren, count it all joy
when you fall into various trials,
knowing that the testing of your faith produces patience.

But let patience have its perfect work,
that you may be perfect and complete lacking nothing.'
- James 1:2-4 -

god se ek was dood
gister middag maar
hy het nog 'n plan
en n werk vir my. Jesus
se ek besoek die hemel
gereeld god se het nee, jou
werk is nog nie klaar nie.

> *God says I was almost dead yesterday, but He still has a plan*
> *for my life and a job for me to do. Jesus says I visit heaven*
> *often. God says my work is not finished.*

Back at Hartebeespoort, we took Aldo to the doctor again. They only increased his medication and shrugged their shoulders; there is no 'wonder-pill' for epilepsy. Without a solution, we were sent back home.

I know we are not fighting against flesh and blood, but the principalities of the air (see Ephesians 6:12). In his weak physical condition Aldo is also vulnerable in his soul dimension and that is exactly when the enemy tries to attack. The enemy will always target the weak and dry areas in our lives – when we are weak and struggle to fight back, we become a target for his arrows. The Bible warns us: *'Be sober, be vigilant; because your adversary the devil walks about like a roaring lion, seeking whom he may devour. Resist him, steadfast in the faith, knowing that the same sufferings are experienced by your brotherhood in the world'* (1 Peter 5:8-9).

I fasted, and prayed, and called out to God; and through it all I died to myself more and more. There were many nights when I just paced in front of Aldo's bed and spoke the Word of God over him. Even though he is a teenager, his bed is now next to mine because we need to react quickly when an epileptic attack comes. When he breaths a few loud breaths, the light is on and everyone is awake and concerned. Fear then threatens to take hold of us, so we first have to break the spirit of fear, plead the blood of Jesus, and then try to go back to sleep. This is how we spent many nights fighting between life and death.

Waarom sien julle hom
hie. hy soek my lewe
en ek sal nie ungee nie.

> *Why can't you see him? He wants to take my life,*
> *but I won't give in!*

Because Aldo's spiritual eyes are wide open, he can detect the enemy even though I can't see him with my natural eyes. During this time, I constantly battled with the feeling of failure. The epileptic attacks made me feel as if my hands were tied behind my back, and there was nothing I could do to help my son. All that was left was to be a mother of faith who covers him with a song of praise.

hulle wil my probeer moedeloos maak.

> *They are trying to make me lose hope.*

I have prayed for people all over the world. I have seen cancer healed, lame children walking, and many other kinds of miraculous healings by the hand of God, but my own child still fights for his life on a daily basis.

'What am I doing wrong, Jesus?' I wondered in frustration.

'Retha,' comes His faithful response, 'true faith is found in those who praise Me for the victory long before the victory materializes. When your faith gets tested, it's not *your* ability being tested, but rather My faithfulness being proved. Every trial you go through is to prove My faithfulness and to reveal My character. When you surrender the trial unto Me and persevere until the end, you will never be disappointed. Will you surrender your life to Me, so I can be glorified through you? The reward of your faith will be another song of praise. But then you won't sing of the miracle that is coming, you will sing of the miracle that took place. I am Faithful and True.'

I refuse to murmur about the desert or fear the great big ocean. I will sing praises to God for the hidden wonders, waiting to be discovered, just beyond the surface of what I can see. My reality is not what I can see, but the Word of God. I won't give up hope, I will keep on believing – *because Jesus is alive!*

> *My heart is hurting because I am so confused.*
> *What is wrong with me? Jesus says He has already died for my healing. I love you, Mom.*
> *God says He will give you strength for what we are going through now. You are a pillar in my life. Jesus told me He is truly faithful and He asks if we will show the world that He is alive? His love for us is very big.*
> *Do you love Him as I love Him?*
> *My help comes from Jesus.*

Spiritual warfare

mamma jy en pappa
is al wat ek het.
Jesus het vir my
gesê god het my so
lief hy het nog baie
werk vir my. God wys
hom hy hou my styf vas
teen sy bors hier die
is teen bose magte wat
my v.

> *Mommy, you and Daddy are all I have. Jesus told me God
> loves me and that He still has a lot of work for me to do.
> God shows me He is holding me tightly against His breast.
> This fight is against the evil forces of the air.*

I am still struggling to decide which is worse: the side effects of the epilepsy or the actual attack. Each one is extremely difficult, but on a different level. The actual attack is violent, lasting only a few moments, whereas the side effects can drag on for weeks.

The first telltale sign of the epilepsy is Aldo's confusion. He gets so confused some days that I wonder if he even knows where he is. The other side effects are aggression and frustration.

Through these attacks, the Lord has taught me to constantly pray in my spirit. I have discovered the art of praying in my heavenly language anywhere, anyplace. Like Paul said in Ephesians 6:18, *'praying always with all prayer and supplication in the Spirit, being watchful to this end with all perseverance and supplication for all the saints....'*

In Second Timothy 3, the Church is given an indication of what to expect in the last days. Satan brings opposition, trials, trouble, and tribulation to separate believers from God in the hope that their love will grow cold toward God and toward each other. If we intend to be victorious in our walk through life, we must be prepared to stand strong when the storms of life hit – not with a strength that comes from ourselves; but we must be strong in the Lord, strong in faith, and strong in perseverance. God is looking for people who are willing to be transformed by the wilderness season. Our goal should be to keep standing on the inside, with our spirit anchored in God's Word, knowing He will take care of the battle raging on the outside. All we need to do is to keep our foothold on the Rock, and then God will do what we can't do (see Ephesians 6:13).

After another one of his attacks, Aldo wrote:

Wat maak hy hier
God wil my gesond
hê hy is nou hier
by ons, Sy naam
is Lusifer hy wil
my dood hê

> *What is he doing here?*
> *God wants to heal me, but he is now here.*
> *His name is Lucifer, and he wants me dead.*
> *Mommy, please hold me tightly...*

109

Shocked, I read his letter. What is Lucifer doing in my house? Why does he want to kill my child? We are children of God. How can he be allowed in here?

I realized once again that the enemy was cast down on earth, and that he is out to kill, steal, and destroy.

Then and there, I decided to put on my heavenly armor and fight the good fight of faith. I was determined to close every door through which the enemy could have gained entry.

At evening time when most other households watch sitcoms on television, the McPhersons prepare for war. When Aldo goes to bed, little Josh kneels before his bed to pray for him. In his childlike trust, he has become the faith-warrior of the house. We put worship music on that plays continually throughout the night, and we have communion as often as we need it. We know we are not wrestling against flesh and blood, but against the powers and principalities of the air, so we have to fight with spiritual weapons (see Ephesians 6:12). I take my Sword in my hand, which is the Word of God, and I walk up and down in front of Aldo's bed and proclaim Scriptures over him. If his body starts shaking, I shake him right back out of the grip of the enemy with my words: 'Satan, in the name of Jesus, you are not allowed to touch Aldo! No weapon formed against us shall prosper (see Isaiah 54:17). You have no right to Aldo. He belongs to Jesus!'

Tinus and I took turns being the watchman on the wall. I did not dare tell anybody on the outside of the battles raging in our house. Wasn't I also one of those raising my eyebrows at the talk of demons and spiritual battles? I realized that the enemy can sense the high calling on Aldo's life, and that is why he attacks his weak and dry areas, to try and sabotage God's plan.

One morning after one of these fights, Aldo wrote:

Ma'am, your help comes from God.
You chased him away from me. He cannot stay where

110

Aldo was totally confused and disorientated during this period of his life. He would be aggressive and stubborn, even hurting those closest to him; not at all like the Aldo we know and love. I held on to his letters for dear life, because only in his letters did I get to see the heart of the real Aldo.

His body was sick, his soul weak, but his spirit was alive and safely hidden in Christ. I cried before God and once again brought my petition to the King: 'Jesus, please bring Aldo's body, soul, and spirit in line with Your Word. I know most other people would have given up on him by now, but I can't, Lord. If I give up on Aldo now, it would be as if I give up hope in You. Please, Jesus, please…'

I had to leave for America to speak at a conference, and I left Tinus to take care of a very sick young man. As we drove to the airport, Aldo wanted to jump out while the car was idling at the traffic light. We decided it would be better to keep the doors of the house locked for the next few days, to keep Aldo from hurting himself. At the airport, Aldo was so confused he couldn't even remember my name. I boarded that airplane still praying and crying, 'Please, Lord Jesus! Please hear my petition.'

When people ask us how Aldo is doing, Tinus and I always give an answer of faith. 'All is well. God is in control,' we say. Even if our son is not doing well at all, our faith is not in his outward condition, but in God's faithfulness. We know God is not a man that He should lie, and He will complete the work He started in Aldo.

God says He loves me. He held me close the whole night,

> *and He chased away that which wanted to hurt me.*
> *Jesus said through reading the Word you opened the*
> *way for Him. Do you want to know what He said?*
> *He said He is the only God and He will heal me.*
> *God wants you to trust Him, because He will do what*
> *He said. You are a big threat to the demons.*

In God's school of the Spirit we learn through practical experience. I had to go back to the Bible and study how Jesus handled His personal confrontations with the enemy, in order to be victorious. Yes, there are many books I could have read, or courses I could have taken, but I chose to follow my Rabbi (Teacher) the best way I know how – by following His example. I don't want more dogma, but the revealed truth of God's Word. God Himself taught me how to handle every confrontation with the enemy.

This scripture anchored my faith:

> 'And these signs will follow those who believe:
> In My name they will cast out demons;
> they will speak with new tongues;
> they will take up serpents; and if they drink anything deadly,
> it will by no means hurt them;
> they will lay hands on the sick, and they will recover.'
> *- Mark 16:17-18 -*

Although extremely painful, these spiritual battles sent my ministry into a completely new level. God will use everything the enemy means for evil and turn it into something good for His glory, if we let Him.

The first time I realized I had moved into a new level in my walk with God, was when I ministered in Asia. Eastern countries are renowned for the wide variety of religions practiced there. You are openly confronted with anything from Buddhism, Hinduism, and atheism, to Christianity. As I sat on the airplane, thinking about what was waiting for me, and the spiritual atmosphere I was soon about to encounter, I asked God to open my spiritual eyes so I could discern the spirits and fight effectively with my heavenly armor.

A day or two later as I was preaching at a big revival meeting, the glory of God fell on us. Suddenly, people started reacting strangely as the light of God exposed the darkness. Some made snake-like movements or gawked like chickens. I was astonished! I called to Jesus to help me, because I had never seen anything like this before and had no idea what to do next. There were a lot of Buddhists and Moslems in the crowd, but I experienced the Holy Spirit saying: 'Don't judge, Retha. Even Christians struggle with demonic strongholds or manifestations. My grace, My freedom, My love is there for everyone.'

> '…Those who are well have no need of a physician,
> but those who are sick.
> I did not come to call the righteous, but sinners, to repentance.'
> *- Mark 2:17 -*

Christians can also open doors to the enemy through things like: unforgiveness, bitterness, hatred, rejection, fear, word curses, and other ungodly things we expose ourselves to. We must be especially careful what we let in through our eyes and our ears. If we open these doors to the enemy, demons will try to torment us in our weak and dry areas. There will be no real victory in our lives until all the gateways of our body, soul, and spirit are given over to Holy Spirit and under His control. If we give the demons access through these open gateways, they will try to establish strongholds in certain areas of our lives (usually where we are most vulnerable). That is why we have to guard our hearts with all diligence and allow Holy Spirit to work with, and heal, our places of vulnerability.

> 'Keep your heart with all diligence,
> for out of it spring the issues of life.'
> *- Proverbs 4:23 -*

A person might feel extremely oppressed or depressed, not knowing where these emotions come from. This might well be the result of word curses (negative bindings spoken by someone else, or yourself, over your life). We must be careful what we let in through our eyes and ears, but even more vigilant to guard what comes out of our mouths.

In Aldo's case, God revealed to me that he opened a door to the enemy through rejection. The enemy is sneaky when it comes to finding access into our lives. That is why it is so important that we submit all areas of our lives to Holy Spirit. When He guards the gates of our heart, He will immediately sound the alarm if these gates are in danger. It is only through repentance and the blood of Jesus that we can seal these gateways to the enemy. God gave us the greatest weapon of all to defeat the enemy, and that is His love. To find this love we need humility. Our battles will be fought and won on our knees, in total dependence on the King, and absolute obedience to His commands.

> 'When a strong man, fully armed, guards his own palace, his goods are in peace. But when a stronger than he comes upon him and overcomes him, he takes from him all his armor in which he trusted, and divides his spoils.'
> - Luke 11:21-22 -

To heal the sick and to set the captives free was a huge part of Jesus' ministry. We should learn from our Rabbi and follow in His footsteps, not skeptically lifting an eyebrow when these subjects are addressed.

> *You want to forget the past because you got hurt.*
> *God has called you and He loves you very much.*
> *You mustn't give up now. You must listen to Jesus*
> *because He will teach you how to please Him.*
> *I will be what Jesus has planned for me.*
> *Just keep on believing. What I am going through now*

> *is because they want to kill me.*
> *They tried to strangle me,*
> *but Jesus saved me by strangling them.*

The victory we hold over the evil one lies in the blood of the Lamb. Jesus guaranteed our victory through the cross—His sacrifice, His blood, and His resurrection. All the power we need is found in Jesus.

Jesus se ons hoef nie
bekommerd te wees nie
wys my waar is bevryding
wie bevry anders het die
bloed bevry mamma

> *Jesus shows me we don't have to worry about anything.*
> *He shows me where we will find freedom from captivity.*
> *Only the blood will free us.*

Satan is our accuser (see Revelation 12:10), and through his accusations he attempts to paralyze the army of God through guilt, shame, unbelief, and fear. His aim is to keep us in bondage. Just like Pharaoh refused to let the Israelites go, so too Satan wants to keep the children of God from their inheritance and destiny in God. He wants to keep us from the abundant life Jesus promised, and he enters and manipulates our lives when we open doors to him through the choices we make. We can't afford to be ignorant of the enemy's schemes, but we should never lose sight of the victory Jesus guaranteed for us on the cross.

> *God shows me how the demons are out to kill me.*

> *Get behind me, Satan! He wants to confuse me,*
> *but he won't win!*

Here are a few tactics the enemy can use to gain access into a believers life:

The first and most probably most serious is **unforgiveness**. Harboring unforgiveness in your heart is a most dangerous trap of the enemy, because it disqualifies you from God's forgiveness of your sins. Remember the parable Jesus told of the attendant whose large debt was cancelled by the master, yet he was unwilling to cancel the small amount his fellow attendant owed to him (see Matthew 18:23-35). In the end, he was disqualified from his master's mercy because of his own inability to extend mercy to others. Unforgiveness literally robs you of your forgiveness and grace. **Forgiveness** closes many of the open doors the enemy could use to kill, steal and destroy. Forgiveness is a choice not an emotion – God's grace will do the rest.

Bitterness has its root in unforgiveness. Bitterness is the gall you drink hoping someone else will get sick, but only poisoning yourself in the process. Bitterness chains you to the past. You will never be free to stretch yourself out to the beautiful future that God has planned for you if you foster bitterness and unforgiveness in your heart.

Rejection is another fiery arrow that cripples many. Rejection can also open doors to sexual immorality and lust. The enemy will use your feelings of unworthiness against you, to make you seek your self-worth in all the wrong places.

Any **addiction** is an open door. Addiction is anything to which you devote the time, energy, or affection that rightfully belongs to God. Addiction is not limited to the extreme cases such as drugs, alcohol, or sex, but can also be your hobby, your body, or even television soap operas or video games.

Fear is a sneaky trap. Through trauma or dramatic events we become easy targets, because then we are usually emotionally or physically vulnerable. The moment you recognize the workings of fear in your life, you need to cast it out! The Word of God says in Second Timothy 1:7, *'God has not given us a spirit of fear, but of power and of love and of a sound mind.'* God has made the way for you to live your life in complete freedom from fear. It is there for all of us – Jesus promised peace, not fear. We must keep on seeking this peace and not give up until every area of our lives is filled with His peace.

I minister in many schools, and wherever I go I see the work of the enemy amongst our children. Alcohol, drugs, pornography, lust, and sexual immorality are the result of the spiritual apathy and negligence of the previous generations. Harry Potter has opened a door to witchcraft in even the most innocent of children's bedrooms, and the wonder-working power of the Holy Spirit is replaced by fantasy and dark arts. The problem is that through our criticism and unbelief, the gifts and the workings of the Holy Spirit are not always welcome in our churches anymore. Our children need to be brought back to the power and freedom that is found only in Jesus Christ.

> *You were right the whole time; I don't want to hurt you!*
> *Jesus says I must use communion.*

The blood of the Lamb has guaranteed us the victory, but the doors still need to be closed through our repentance.

> 'Truly, these times of ignorance God overlooked,
> but now commands all men everywhere to repent.'
> *- Acts 17:30 -*

Repentance is not an emotion, but a choice. Through sincere repentance, we humble ourselves before God and seek His mercy. This will close the door to the enemy and will pave the way for God to change our hearts. Before we can take communion, we must search our hearts and turn toward God through repentance. Just as a fish needs water to live, so the enemy needs darkness. The blood of the Lamb is the light that will drive out all darkness. The Bible gives us this amazing promise if we should sincerely turn away from sin, toward God:

> 'If My people who are called by My name
> will humble themselves, and pray and seek My face,
> and turn from their wicked ways, then I will hear from heaven
> and will forgive their sin and heal their land.'
> *- 2 Chronicles 7:14 -*

God has given us everything to walk as victors against our adversary, but this doesn't mean the fight is going to be easy. We are not going to win the fight if we live from spiritual milk only. We have to grow up in the things of the Lord and fill ourselves with meat from the Bible.

> 'For everyone who partakes only of milk is
> unskilled in the word of righteousness, for he is a babe.
>
> But solid food belongs to those who are of full age,
> that is, those who by reason of use have their senses
> exercised to discern both good and evil.'
> *- Hebrewes 5:13-14 -*

I have come to a place in my life where the desire to please God has completely overshadowed the temptation to please man. I have decided to keep myself deaf to the criticism of those who don't agree with my direct approach to spiritual warfare. I think that is the reason the enemy has gone undetected in our lives – people are too scared of what others may think or say. 'Don't you think you are taking this too seriously, Retha?'

No! We must put on the armor of God and resist the enemy.

> 'You therefore must endure hardship
> as a good soldier of Jesus Christ.
> No one engaged in warfare entangles himself
> with the affairs of this life, that he may please him
> who enlisted him as a soldier.'
> *- 2 Timothy 2:3-4 -*

From all my encounters with demons, I have come to this conclusion: we are at war! Sometimes an arrow will hit, and then we feel hurt and defeated. We shouldn't give up – God gave us a shield of faith and the sword of the Spirit to fight back.

The more we fight, the stronger we become and the wiser we are to the enemy's tactics. We will only taste the victory if we stay close to our Commander and live in His light.

The precious blood of Jesus has purchased the victory. Satan's intent was to literally kill, steal, and destroy in Aldo's life, but the Truth has set him free. Now he is free indeed! Praise God!

Jesus says what happened to me was the demons tried to kill me. Did you know where I was, was truly a terrible place to be. They strangled me all the time, but I am free now. I gave my heart to Jesus and He helped me when they tried to hurt me. Jesus strangled them with His hands. It is because I have such an important job I have to do for Jesus.

My life belongs to Jesus

Jesus se jy het hom
vertrou en hy het ons
worsteling gesien daarom
het hy wysheid vir my
gegee. het jy geweet
wie Jesus liefhe en sod
eer en die Heilige gees
een word
het wat jy hom gee
kan hy verander. God se
hy het reeds vir ons lewe
gegee van een as asb my
lewe behoort aan Jesus
moenie my terug vut nie

Jesus says you trusted Him, and He sees all our struggles.
That is why He has given me wisdom. You must love Jesus,
honor God, and become one with the Holy Spirit.
Only what you give Him, He can change. God says He has
already given us life. My life belongs to Jesus.
Please don't ever take me back, Mommy.

For most people in South Africa, December is holiday time. During the year I am away from home a lot, and that is why our annual family holiday at Yzerfontein (a small holiday town on the west coast of South Africa) is so special to me. At the end of 2008, I knew the summer holiday was going to hold its challenges, because Aldo was still very sick, but I hoped that the fresh ocean air and well-deserved rest would do us all some good.

With the mini-bus filled to maximum capacity, we set off to the Cape. The team consisted of Dad Tinus and Mom Retha in the front seats, and Aldo and Josh in the back seats with their cousins, Sammy and Elisma. Katie and Regina, the two ladies who work for us, also squeezed in. In addition to these, we had one dog – Moya; two birds – Mercy and Grace, and a legion of angels to protect us. The last things to be packed were Aldo's oxygen bottle and medication (not a pleasant sight, but my hopes were still high), and finally we were off!

On the way there, my dream started to crumble as reality set in. While on the road, Aldo started acting strange. We thought he was going to kick out the windows of the minibus at the rate he was going on. At that stage, we didn't know he was reacting to his physical pain, we just thought it might be the signs of another spiritual battle beginning. I mentally prepared myself for what I knew was coming, and I starting praying in the Spirit and confessing Scriptures over and over.

We arrived at Yzerfontein late that night, and we were all relieved that the road trip was finally over. I am ashamed to say this, but I couldn't wait to get to the safety of our home, lock the door behind us, and keep Aldo away from the rest of the world. He was in such a state that we could no longer take him anywhere. Our holiday home became our hiding place.

At the start of the new week, Tinus had to fly back to Hartebeespoort to finish the last of his work at the office. He would join us again over the weekend, and so I was once again alone with the kids for the week.

We carried a mattress into our room so Aldo could sleep next to our bed, but there were a lot of sleepless nights that holiday. Aldo was talking to himself, or into the air, most of the time. He didn't recognize us or even remember our names. Josh and the girls tried to entertain him in the mornings by playing his favorite games, but he just became irritated and aggressive. The longer the day wore on, the more out of control the situation became.

Aldo was not interested in going to the beach or playing games. He would lie down on the floor anywhere in the house and refuse to get up. He didn't want to eat, and lost a lot of weight in a very short time. The longer we were shut in at the house, the more frustrated he became. He had no balance, no bladder control, and what disturbed me the most was that he would pound his head against the wall.

After a few days of 'house arrest,' I felt like I couldn't take it longer. I asked Katie to look after him for a little while, and I ran down to the beach, Bible in hand. I fell to my knees in the sand and cried out to Jesus, 'Jesus! I can see Aldo is dying. Surely, You must see it, too, Lord. Where are You?' I felt like one of the disciples in the boat with Jesus, storm-tossed and afraid, while Jesus slept peacefully in the front of the boat. Just like the disciples, I wanted to wake up the Lord and ask: 'Can't You see that we are perishing, Lord!' (see Luke 8:23-25).

I took the Bible in my hand and loudly declared into the heavens, 'Lord, I know You are the God of Abraham, Isaac, and Jacob, the eternal God who always fulfills His promises. If You should choose to take Aldo home now, I will still love You.' I stared at my clenched fist and I remembered God's promise in detail. 'But I know what You promised, and that Your promises can't fall to the ground. Once again, I surrender him to You. Please, Lord. I need a miracle!'

Then I cried and cried until the sand became a pool of tears beneath my hands. Suddenly, a thought flashed through my mind...*I don't want to live anymore. I don't think I can take one more day of this...*

I shuddered at the thought and immediately rebuked myself, 'Come now, Retha. Pull yourself together! Time to get up, dust off, and face a new day.'

I walked back to the house, but this time I walked very slowly. The wind blew my tear-streaked cheeks dry. The pain of seeing my son hurting like this was eating me up on the inside. Feeling downcast, I walked to the back door.

Everything was quiet in the house. This was strange, because normally you could hear Aldo talking to himself. I walked up the stairs to the room where I last saw him. I opened the door to find Aldo and Katie writing. For the prior week, he hadn't wanted to write anything, so this surprised me.

> *You mustn't stop your life! God will heal me.*
> *I want to see you happy again.*
> *Show me how much you love me and stand up.*
> *I can see you don't want to live anymore.*
> *You have so much pain when I am not well.*
> *God says you truly want to see me well again. He says*
> *what is happening to me is that my brain has fluid on it.*
> *He is who He should be. He is God, and He will heal me.*

Each word hit me like a wave.

Aldo knew that I just thought that I didn't want to live anymore? Only God could have revealed this to him in the Spirit.

What is this about fluid on the brain?

I immediately phoned my husband, 'There is fluid on Aldo's brain, Tinus. We need to get him to a doctor!' There was a pause on the other side of the receiver. A bit surprised, Tinus replied, 'How do you know that?' I stumbled over my words, but in short sentences I told him, 'Aldo just wrote it. Please call the doctor in Cape Town and find out when is the soonest that I can bring him in.' Before putting down the phone (with my heart pounding with joy and excitement), I yelled, 'Jesus is alive!'

The first available opening was at nine o'clock the following morning. Early the next day, Regina, Aldo, and I were on the road from Yzerfotein to Cape Town. The hospital was about an hour's drive away. Aldo once again started kicking at the windows, but Regina calmed him down while I focused on the road, praying the whole time. The drive felt like an eternity, but I was full of hope, because I knew there was a breakthrough waiting.

I kept thinking about what he wrote the previous night:

> *What is happening now is that I will be healed.*
> *He says what is going on is that my brain is swollen,*
> *and I have water on my brain.*
> *My God says I have water on my brain.*
> *Please know I will feel better because you are taking me*
> *to a man of God.* (the doctor).
> *I am very sorry. I don't want to hurt you again.*
> *Do you know that God has all your tears in a bottle?*
> *Show Him you will trust Him with my life.*
> *Did you take your work to Him, too?*
> *Because He says He will help you with the book.*

In my human wisdom, I wanted to finish writing this book in December; but God had other plans. Throughout everything that happened, I still tried to write, but I didn't have the time or energy. Taking the advice I usually give to others, I surrendered my problem to God.

'Lord,' I prayed, 'please grant me the strength, the wisdom, and the time to finish this book. Let it be a blessing unto You, and Your name be glorified through it.'

What a confirmation from God for Aldo to write such a letter at the lowest point in his life. This just showed me, again, how God cares about the smallest detail of our lives.

When we finally reached the hospital, Aldo was immediately wheeled in for scans. The Xrays clearly showed the water on his brain, and the doctors decided to do an emergency operation to relieve the pressure. They inserted a shunt from his brain to his stomach to drain the fluid that had built up.

After the operation he was visibly better, although still very weak. From ICU, we took him home, and I had new hope for the holiday. We realized that Jesus once again saved his life – even if it was at number ninety-nine, He wasn't too late. Later Aldo told me about the angels he saw in the operating room and that Jesus was there with him the whole time.

At home he grew stronger by the day, and I knew the Lord answered my prayer for a miracle. The water on his brain caused intense pressure and headaches and this was the reason for his epileptic attacks (since then, Aldo hasn't had another attack, praise God!).

> *God says you gave your life to Him.*
> *What happened is what happens*
> *to some people who have injuries to the brain.*
> *My head is feeling much better, and it doesn't hurt at all.*
> *God says the water that made me so sick is off now.*
> *I will now get better, faster and faster.*
> *God says He knows how sick I was.*
>
> *I went with Him to heaven again last night and*
> *He showed me the life that is waiting for me.*
> *God says you trust Him, and He shows me how we*
> *minister together. You are so good to me.*

The result of the operation was truly miraculous! Aldo immediately started eating again, he regained control of his bladder, and he could walk on his own because his balance was better. Words cannot describe the thanksgiving I felt for this relative return to normality. The confusion and disorientation were now the only giants left to fight, but I put my trust in God and the power of His Word. For what God starts, He will finish!

> *I was confused at first because I had so much pain,*
> *but now I don't have pain anymore.*
> *I am confused now because*
> *my head got hurt with all the water on my brain.*

> *Please believe me when I tell you that what*
> *is happening to me now is only temporary.*
> *God says I will definitely be healed.*
> *Do not worry. God said you trusted Him,*
> *and He will heal me.*
> *Ma'am, God says, you and*
> *I should be as He showed me we will be.*
> *God says I will minister across the world.*

Once home, the rest of the family hesitantly gave a sigh of relief, while still carefully keeping an eye on Aldo. At first everything went smoothly, but after a few days the old symptoms returned. Once again he pounded his head against the wall, he didn't sleep or eat much, he lost control of his bladder, and he was completely off balance. We were back where we started. I couldn't believe it! What went wrong? We did everything according to the doctor's orders.

'What is going on, Jesus?' I asked confused.

hy is weer baie baie
seer. Jesus se wat met
my aangaan is water
is nog nie weg nie. God
se mev. hulle moet
my pompie stel water
moet vinniger uit wysheid
sê ek sal heeltemal gesond
wees. Wens so

> *My head is hurting again. Jesus says what is going*
> *on with me is the water is not gone yet. God says, Ma'am,*
> *they must reset my pump. Water must drain faster.*
> *Wisdom says I will be completely healed. I hope so.*

Once again, we jumped in the car and hastily made our way to the hospital. Thankfully, Tinus was with me this time. The medical team immediately took scans of Aldo's brain, and then wheeled him in for another operation. For the second time that month, I sat praying in the waiting room.

The shunt malfunctioned. The tubes of the shunt diverting the water from his brain to his stomach were blocked. The water couldn't drain effectively, and once again accumulated and caused great pressure on the brain.

After the operation, the doctors kept him for observation a few more days. On the day before Christmas we finally headed home.

23 Desember – Aldo after operation in ICU.

Liewe mamma en pappa
ek is nou weer baie
beter weet julle Jesus
en die engele was
nou in die teater.
Weet sy ek sal nou
met so n spoed gesond
word my werk gaan
nou segin.
Jesus wil my nou
hemel toe vat ek
ek sal later skryf.

Dear Mommy and Daddy, I feel a lot better. Jesus and the angels were in the theatre with me! I will be healed now at great speed and begin with my work.

Once home, a week went by without any incidents. Everyone began to relax and tried to enjoy what little part of the holiday was left. Now that Aldo was so much better, this was finally within reach!

December drew to a close and as we started making preparations for our return home, I woke up one morning to see the old glazed expression in Aldo's eyes.

'No, no, no! What is going on, Aldo? Do you feel OK?' I asked with a twinge of hopelessness in my voice.

> *You must know that what is happening now is*
> *I am being healed. It looks like you want to give up hope.*
> *Do you know how I feel when you look like you want to give*
> *up hope? I only have you, and you have Jesus.*
> *You know you can't give up!*
> *Jesus showed you Himself* (what is going to happen).
> *Please, don't give up hope. Just keep on believing!*

Later he wrote:

Liefste
mamma weet jy ek sal
met oop arms wen god se
wat met my nou gebeur
my wond het infeksie

> *Dear Mommy, do you know I am going to win this race!*
> *God says what is happening now*
> *is my wound has infection*
> *and my body doesn't want to accept it.*

I phoned the doctor, and he confirmed that it is not uncommon for a patient's body to reject foreign objects, like a shunt. He prescribed a strong dose of antibiotics and told us it was nothing to worry about. In a flash, the confusion disappeared as the antibiotics started working.

> *Do you know, I really hope that what is wrong with me will stop now. Do you know how much it hurts me when you cry all the time? God catches all your tears.*
> *I love you, Mommy, and you know that I am not always myself.*

After six weeks of continual knee-time in prayer, I entered into a new level of intimacy with the King. In those times of seeking the Lord with all my heart, I discovered new treasures in His presence. As we drove back to Hartebeespoort, I held on to two stones bearing inscriptions: *God is faithful* in my right hand and *God is never late* in my left hand. I know these gems are of immeasurable worth, because it cost a lot of tears and faith to find them. I will never let go of these treasures. They are mine forever. Whenever I feel discouraged, I just look at the treasures in my hands again and I hold on to what God has given me. That is revelation knowledge – something real and tangible, even though it can't be seen with the natural eye.

> *God says He knows what is going to happen now and that I have His wisdom. God shows me the water on my brain is gone. God says I will be healed quickly now. Just be patient. He knows my time for work has started. Please read the Bible to me; I have to start reading. He says He knows I will start quickly.*
> *Do you know that my head isn't hurting anymore? Be prepared. God will show you that Wisdom and I work together. Be prepared any moment, because I am just going to stand up one day. He was here a little while ago.*
> *He says you love Him very much, Mommy.*

We started off 2009 like most other families, by packing lunch boxes for both our sons for their first day of school. Three weeks earlier, I didn't have much hope for this day dawning. Once again, I lift up my hands in worship and read the inscription on the stones: *'Yes, Lord. You are faithful; and thank You, Jesus, for never being late!'*

god se by

h om is alles m o o n t lik

God says with Him everything is possible!

'For with God nothing will be impossible.'
- Luke 1:37 -

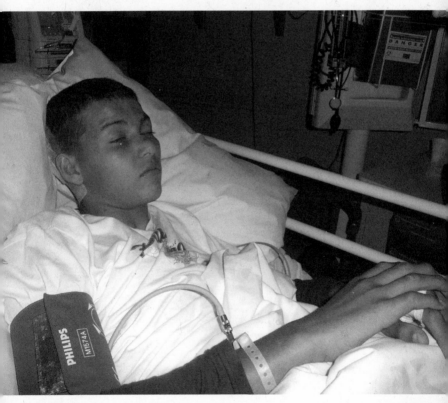

Aldo after the operation

Josh, Aldo, Sammy, and Elisma

The cloud called Grace

God se
Jy is baie seer, sal jy glo
ek sal gesond word.
lewe net vir Jesus
wysheid wys my dat
my kop met my lyf
een sal word. god se
my lewe sal wees soos
Povlus wat ook die
3e hemel gesien het. Weet
jy ek wil julle so graag
g?lukkig sien. mev ek
weet jy het seer en ook
pappa daarom die stryery
wees net soos wat Jesus
was die minste.

God says you are hurting.
Will you keep on believing
I will be healed? Only live for Jesus.
Wisdom shows me my head will come in line
with the rest of my body.
God says my life will be like Paul's life who
saw the third heaven. I want to see you happy again.
Ma'am, I know you and Daddy are hurting
and that is the reason for the arguments.
Just be like Jesus shows me – the least.

'Lord, I am a woman who dares to take You at Your Word. I will stand on Your Word and trust You unconditionally. Your promises and faithfulness are now my reality.'

This was my prayer when I stood next to Aldo's hospital bed, at the beginning of this supernatural journey.

Now, after five years, I heard myself asking God for a sign to confirm His promises.

One night while praying and just sharing my heart with Jesus, I unexpectedly asked Him if He would give me a sign that it is really His plan to heal Aldo completely.

'Lord,' I said, 'You know my greatest desire for Aldo is to see his spirit, soul, and flesh in line with Your Word. Please, Jesus. Will You confirm that You are going to heal and restore him fully, so that he can do the work You sent him to do?'

I am somewhat ashamed to admit to this prayer, because I know it is impossible to please God without faith. Asking for a sign felt like 'doubt' to me, and I believe in unconditional faith; because I know God loves me with unconditional love.

Later, while drinking a cup of tea and speaking with Holy Spirit, I thought about my request. 'Please, Lord. Forgive me for questioning You. You don't have to give me a sign; I choose to trust You unconditionally. Our lives are in Your hands.' And I reminded myself: *'The Lord maintains my lot'* (see Psalm 16:5).

God says He sees your heart. I will be as wise as Solomon.
Be prepared. He shows me how I minister in front
of thousands of people.
Did you know you will get the gift you asked of God –
my spirit, soul, and flesh in line with God's Word?

And in another one of his letters, he wrote:

God said you asked Him, Jesus,
and the Holy Spirit for wisdom.
Jesus says He will give you God-given help.
He says you asked Him if I will be healed.
He says, 'Yes.' You will be very happy.
Jesus says you and I will learn that He can be trusted.

And:

> *Jesus says I will be like Moses. I will walk*
> *and talk normally again. Jesus says what is happening*
> *now is how He has planned it – to rain His Spirit*
> *down over people. You must keep on doing what you are*
> *doing. Jesus said you must offer me to God.*
> *God says you are asking a sign if I will be healed.*
> *He said what you asked Him, He will do.*
> *Please believe me when I tell you.*
> *Jesus told me I will be able to do everything*
> *as I did it in the past. Mommy, you will be like*
> *Aimee McPherson. Like she was, you will be.*

When Aldo wrote this letter I thought Aimee McPherson was a long lost relative of Tinus. Later, a friend of mine told me she was a great evangelist in the 1920s and her name was among those listed as 'God's generals.'

Deep inside of me I understand that this road we are walking on with Aldo is part of the purifying process, but in my weakness I sometimes become impatient. I have seen the invisible, tasted the victory, and taken the promise by faith – the problem is that I so desperately want to see the promise fulfilled *now,* in *my* time.

Through the waiting-season I have learned to enjoy life, regardless of the circumstances, and to endure until the end – because I know there is a reward for perseverance. Godly character, wisdom, authority, and fulfilled promises are waiting at the end of the trial.

> 'Blessed…is the man who is patient
> under trial and stands up under temptation,
> for when he has stood the test and been approved,
> he will receive [the victor's] crown of life which God has
> promised to those who love Him.'
> *- James 1:12 AMP -*

Holy Spirit so clearly says to my heart: 'Retha, don't outrun My cloud of grace. Don't run ahead. My anointing is only found under the cloud. The sun will scorch you the moment you move out from under it. Don't let impatience deceive you. Believe Me when I say My timing is perfect.'

In the times when Aldo is sick or confused I want to protect him from the prying eyes of the world. From past hurts, I have learned I can't expect everyone to look at him through eyes of faith as I do. Every time I look at Aldo, I choose to see the potential of what God can do, instead of staring myself blind at what I can't change with my own strength.

After one of my meetings, a beautiful young lady walked up to me and casually said, 'I hope you realize that head injuries only heal up to a certain point. Then, the patient reaches a plateau. Have you given it any thought that Aldo may have reached his plateau by now?' People can hurt more with their words than they ever realize. Through careless words the enemy sows seeds of doubt and confusion.

Driving home that night, my heart was breaking. Weeks after the meeting, I was still thinking about her words. In retrospect, I should have answered her question with a question: 'Tell me, is there a plateau to the wonders God can do?'

Each of us needs to search our heart and ask: Is anything impossible for God? Or have we just reached a plateau in our faith? *For with God **nothing** is ever impossible!*

> *God says His angels must protect us. He makes this*
> *a heavenly road for us, for we will learn to trust only in Him.*
> *God says He is in control.*

Although I often go to pray for people in hospital, I have never felt led to take Aldo with me. It might be that the cloud of grace has never moved in that direction, but for now I wait on God for His perfect timing. When God gives me the green light, I will take Aldo with me when I minister.

Late one Sunday afternoon, our family, accompanied by a pastor friend from America, went to visit a young lady in hospital. She had been lying in a semicoma for a couple of weeks. After I finished praying, my friend suggested that Aldo should also pray. I thought about it for a moment and hesitantly put some anointing oil in Aldo's hand, wondering what to expect next.

To my surprise, he peacefully walked up to her bed, put his hand on her forehead, and started praying in his slow, monotone voice. Suddenly, her stiff body gave a jolt and we sensed that the power of God just went through her in a mighty way. (I don't know who was more surprised – me or our American friend. No one expected to see God's power flow like that.)

As we walked back to the car, the adults were silent, but Aldo went on as if nothing happened – completely childlike in his faith.

God se ek mag al bid vir mense ek het jou gehoor vra wees verseker ek wese hy se mense sal gesond word ek sien hoe ek met my hande mense aanraak wysheid wys my hoe ek vir mense woord gee. Lief vir julle.

> *God says I am allowed to pray for people.*
> *I heard you asking Him. Rest assured,*
> *I know He said people will be healed.*
> *I see how I lay my hands on people.*
> *Wisdom shows me how I give people Word. Love you, Mom.*

The mysteries of God will never stop captivating my heart!

'And He said to me, "My grace is sufficient for you, for My strength is made perfect in weakness." Therefore most gladly I will rather boast in my infirmities, that the power of Christ may rest upon me.'
- 2 Corinthians 12:9 -

God says you are scared of what the people are going to say. His work in me is very big. Just know the wisdom I have, God gives me. **He wants everybody to be saved.** God will let me be as I was in the past, only better.

I have learned that God doesn't have to prove Himself. We only have to look up into the starry sky He created, to know He is sovereign and almighty. It is because of His amazing love toward us and His cloud of grace, that we can face each new day. God is good, His ways are perfect, and He is always on time. He can accomplish His master plan anyway He wants – His wisdom is so much higher than what we can understand.

Thank You, Lord, for using the foolish to teach the wise; and for Your cloud of grace, so we can dwell in the shadow of the Almighty!

The winds of change are blowing

(24 Des 2008) Vandag uit ICU.
Kaap.

Jesus se ek sal nou
vinnig gesond word.
Mev ek weet ek
wat gaan gebeur ek
weet ek gaan net opstaan
en begin bedien eers moet
ek heeltemal gesond
word nou. hy se ek
moet net heeltemal
hom vertrou ek sal want
ek weet ek het hom
gesien en hy is werklik
god ek en jy sal
regtig saam bedien ek
weet werklik ek hoef
nie bekommerd te wees nie
god en ek was weer mev
by engele weet ek en Jesus
was by water waar hy
my weer vertel het van
wat gaan gebeur ek weet
my bediening het begin
bevestig ek en jy sal saam
bedien. god se jy weet ek
is Sy profeet en jy eer
my.

> *Jesus says my healing will be quick. Ma'am, I know what*
> *is going to happen – I know I will one day stand up*
> *and start ministering. But first I need to recover.*
> *He says I must trust Him completely.*
> *I will, because I have seen Him, and He is truly God.*
> *You and I will truly minister together.*
> *I know I don't have to be anxious.*
> *God and I were with the angels again.*
> *Jesus and I were by the water where He told me*
> *about what was going to happen.*
> *I know my ministry has started.*
> *God says you know I am His prophet and you honor me.*

Always wondering, from one moment to the next, what Aldo is going to be up to is the most difficult aspect of raising him. He is totally unpredictable. When he sees angels, it doesn't matter who is with him, he will spontaneously react to them. Or, he will fall on his face to worship God where and when he wants. When he is speaking to Jesus, he will tell whoever interrupts him, to wait their turn – and that includes Tinus and me. Come what may, Jesus comes first! To walk in the Spirit is a daily reality for him.

When I am away from home, I try to phone the children every morning before they leave for school, just so I can hear their voices and tell them I love them. One morning, while I was away ministering in Cape Town, I phoned home as I always do. When I spoke to Aldo, he was speaking much slower than he normally does, and this is usually a sign that he didn't get much sleep the previous night.

'What's wrong Aldo?' I asked. 'Talk to Daddy, Mom. It is going to take too long for me to explain.'

After telling him how much I love him, he handed the phone to Tinus. My husband said, 'We didn't sleep a wink last night. Aldo couldn't stop talking about the angel on the wall outside the house. The neighbor's dog kept on barking at the angel, and Aldo wanted to go outside and chase the dog away. I tried my best to keep him in bed, but he wouldn't listen, so we were up most of the night.'

Upon my return, I immediately asked Aldo about the angel. 'What was the angel doing here, Aldo? What did the angel say?' I eagerly wanted to know.

'He brought us a message, Mommy. He said the winds of change are here.'

I don't know if you have felt these winds of change blowing in your own life, but I definitely have. There is a shifting and a sifting in the spirit realm as the winds of change blow, separating the chaff from the wheat. The time is here where the Spirit and the Bride cry out: 'Come, Lord Jesus, come!' These winds of change may unsettle you if your foundation is not firmly and deeply set on the Rock of Ages. Make sure your relationship with Jesus is one of substance and intimacy, not merely religious acts based on tradition and dogma.

There is urgency in Aldo to start ministering to people. He constantly encourages me to keep on working and to be the hands and feet of Jesus: 'Go, Mom! Go and work for Jesus!' I often come home very tired from my speaking engagements. After a few days at home, Aldo will write again:

> *Jesus and Wisdom showed me how you love Him.*
> *He wants to give me Wisdom. Listen.*
> *You must go and work, because Jesus is on His way.*

He is eagerly looking forward to the day when the Lord releases him into the fullness of his ministry. Right from the beginning it has been his greatest desire to work for Jesus. Here is an excerpt from one of his earliest letters:

> *Wish I was healed now. I want to show what I saw in heaven. I saw a lot of angels! Do you know Anton and I had a great time playing together? Do you know when I was with Moses I saw you praying for me?*

> *When are we going to show my letters*
> *to the people that don't believe?*
> *Jesus told me He doesn't want people to be lost. I must tell*
> *them Jesus is alive! He loves people very much.*
> *Do you know we will get through this?*
> *He will never leave us.*
> (Anton was one of the boys Aldo met in heaven.)

Aldo understands the seriousness of the hour we are living in. This knowledge drives the passion in his heart to tell the world: 'Jesus is alive!'

> 'Then He spoke to them a parable:
> "Look at the fig tree, and all the trees.
> When they are already budding, you see and know
> for yourselves that summer is now near.
> So you also, when you see these things happening,
> know that the kingdom of God is near.
> Assuredly, I say to you, this generation will
> by no means pass away till all things take place.
> Heaven and earth will pass away,
> but My words will by no means pass away.
>
> But take heed to yourselves lest your hearts be weighed down
> with carousing, drunkenness, and the cares of this life,
> and that Day come on you unexpectedly.
> For it will come as a snare on all those who dwell
> on the face of the whole earth. Watch therefore,
> and pray always that you may be counted worthy
> to escape all these things that will come to pass,
> and to stand before the Son of Man
> - *Luke 21: 29-36* -

Someone sent a testimony to my office that was written in 1918 by a South African preacher. He also had a near-death experience. His account confirmed a lot of what Aldo told us through his letters. The only difference is, the preacher could tell his story without any restrictions or limitations, because he fully recovered soon after his sickness, whereas Aldo still struggles to talk.

What struck me from the man's testimony was his under-standing of the second heaven. For a South African preacher living in 1918 to talk about the spiritual realm was definitely unusual, and not going to win him a popularity contest. He testified that he saw the elders of his church fervently praying for his health, but some of the prayers were unable to get through to the throne of God. These prayers were hindered for various reasons. Mostly, the prayers were drowned out by the noise of the enemy. If there was willful, unrepented sin in the believer's life, the demons could laugh off the requests sent up to God.

After reading his gripping testimony I prayed more earnestly than ever before: 'Please show me my heart, Lord. Let Your light shine in my heart so that I can repent and come with boldness to Your throne of grace with my prayers.'
I resolved not to go down that same path of praying powerless, ineffective prayers. I want my life to count. I want my prayers to be heard, and most of all, I want to live a holy life so I can be the hands and feet of Jesus here on earth.

The only way to get to this place is to deal with the sin in our lives — not out of our own strength, but by the grace of God and the leading of the Holy Spirit. We need to be willing to turn our back on sin if the Holy Spirit convicts us. We can then repent and be washed with the blood of the Lamb. Unrepented sin not only hinders our prayers, but it also delays our miracles.

Aldo and Miss Patrys spend a large part of their day together. He often goes with her after school when she runs her daily errands and he keeps her company. Miss Patrys' elderly next-door neighbor became extremely sick, and Miss Patrys offered that she and Aldo go over and pray for her. After Miss Patrys finished praying, Aldo also had a turn. He started, 'Lord, please heal this lady eighty percent...no, no, let's make it seventy-five percent...' After a long pause, he finally said, 'OK, Jesus. Please heal her seventy percent.'

When Miss Patrys told me this story, both of us were somewhat surprised by his strange prayer request. We didn't know what to make of it. Later Miss Patrys told me the Holy Spirit spoke to her heart and revealed that her neighbor still had some bitterness in her heart to deal with. The last thirty percent was in her hands and would be determined by the choices she made. Aldo recognized the bitterness, and he knew that she would have to forgive for the fullness of God's healing to come to body, soul, and spirit.

Through this incident, I realized once again that willful, unrepented sin withholds the *fullness* of the blessing from our lives. The Lord wants to heal and restore us one hundred percent, but our choices limit the process. We have a part to play in everything. God waits for our choices, our seeds of faith, our repentance, our willingness to forgive, and our eagerness to live according to His Word; and then He forgives us the way we forgive others.

'For if you forgive men their trespasses, your heavenly Father will also forgive you. But if you do not forgive men their trespasses, neither will your Father forgive your trespasses.'
- *Matthew 6:14-15* -

god wys my weer soos
in die hemel ek sien
hoe almal eintlik eerste
wens is om daar te
bly. god se wie enige
haat in hulle het sal
nie ingaan nie. god se
het my huis weer gewys
my se mer jy het so
groot huis wys my so
huis wat hy vir jou

wil gee wat op see is
hev. Jy moet nou werk
wens hy wil my gou
gesond maak ek wil nie
so anders wees nie.
God se julle sal nie
teleurgestel word nie.

God shows me again what it is like in heaven.
Everyone's first wish is to live there. God says those
who have any hatred inside of them will not go in.
God showed me my house again and I saw that you
also have a big house, Ma'am. He showed me your
house overlooking the ocean. Ma'am, you need to work.
I wish He would heal me soon.
I don't want to be so much different from the rest.
God says you will not be disappointed.

The apostle John was quite clear about this. He said: 'This is the message which we have heard from Him and declare to you, that God is light and in Him is no darkness at all. If we say that we have fellowship with Him, and walk in darkness, we lie and do not practice the truth. But if we walk in the light as He is in the light, we have fellowship with one another, and the blood of Jesus Christ His Son cleanses us from all sin. If we say that we have no sin, we deceive ourselves, and the truth is not in us. If we confess our sins, He is faithful and just to forgive us our sins and to cleanse us from all unrighteousness' (1 John 1:5-9).

The winds of change are busy blowing. Let the wind of the Holy Spirit, the precious Ruach HaKodesh (the Breath, the Wind, the Spirit of God), remove the chaff from the wheat in your life. Don't waste this opportunity to open your heart to God so His wind can blow away what is not of Him and lift you higher into His presence. Allow Him then to lead you and guide you by His Spirit, into the fullness of your divine destiny, as you hear and obey His voice.

> 'The wind blows where it wishes, and you hear the sound of it,
> but cannot tell where it comes from and where it goes.
> So is everyone who is born of the Spirit.'
> *- John 3:8 -*

Aldo and Josh

I suggest you kneel

Hell is the home of the lost soles
What I saw made me cry
Jesus cried with me he said
to me I have to tell everything
I saw. I may not tell you
who I saw he showed me many
who cried to me go and tell
my people hell is real. a man
had a face of a monster
he was a demon. God made
a way for us not to go to hell.
We have to accept Jesus as our
Lord and Savior. he is the way
to the Father. People made noices
they burned with their bodies
Jesus was with me all the time
He want us to be with him
in heavon. Please believe me
hell is for Satan and his
children. he want you to think
that their is not a hell.
Jesus cried and said go and tell
what you saw.

After Aldo woke up from his coma in 2004, he wrote that Jesus showed him heaven and hell. The second part of his statement was very difficult for my natural mind to process. I wondered why Jesus would show hell to a twelve-year-old boy.

During those first few months when he couldn't walk (only crawl somewhat), our family went through a very difficult time that I rarely ever speak about. We were very worried about Aldo. Some nights I thought he was going to climb out the walls the way he was going on. From his letters I understood that his experience in hell was the root of the problem. By God's grace and a lot praying, that season of nightmares, thankfully, also passed.

I know God never does anything without a reason. Sooner or later, His master plan will be understood as the puzzle pieces fall into place. As time went by, he started writing more and more about his experiences in heaven. Many of his earlier writings are recorded in our first book, *A Message From God*, in which he gives detailed descriptions of his heavenly revelations.

Weet mamma
e wige lewe is waar
ons weer saam Jesus
rewe. God op die troon
en Jesus lanks hom

> *Do you know, Mommy, eternal life is where*
> *we live with Jesus again?*
> *God is on the throne and Jesus next to Him.*

He wrote about the children he met there and specifically mentioned two boys close to his age: Dwane and Anton. He wrote letters to each of their parents, consoling them about the loss of their children. He explained how happy they were, and that they didn't want to come back. He even gave us specific instructions of where to find their parents. When we found them exactly as Aldo described, there was no longer any doubt in my mind that his letters were authentic. Till today, I am not moved by worldly reasoning when people try to explain, or discredit, his letters. God is God, and He can do anything!

Only recently it struck me that he has never spoken

much about hell, and I asked him to tell me a bit more. He looked at me with his one eye and said, 'No, Mommy, not now. Jesus said at the precise hour, I will start telling about hell.'

Well, the hour is now here.

Without any prior warning, Aldo began writing in detail about his experiences in hell in December of 2008, after his operations.

> *Jesus said what I must do when I come back is I must tell*
> *the people what I saw and also tell them that Jesus is alive.*
> *I sometimes wish I wasn't taken to hell, because what*
> *I saw there was very bad.*
> *I saw people screaming the whole time.*
>
> *Ma'am, I know that what I saw was very bad.*
> *I was scared, but Jesus and I were both very sad.*
> *I wish I could talk; I want to tell everybody about what*
> *I saw there. Do you know everybody in hell was warned*
> *at some stage, but they didn't want to listen?*
> *God says only repent of your sin and lay it down.*

When I asked him why he suddenly started writing about these experiences, he answered: 'Jesus said in the operating room that I can start telling now. The hour is here.'

There has risen a pressing passion in Aldo to ask everybody he meets, 'Do you know that hell is real?'

> *Do you know who Jesus loves, and who honors God,*
> *and who becomes one with the Holy Spirit?*
> *God can only change what you give Him. Please.*
> *My life belongs to Jesus. Don't take me back.*
> *God showed me hell. I didn't want to look,*
> *but really saw everything. Do you know, Mommy,*
> *what I know you will struggle to believe?*
> *People burn and scream all the time.*

While driving home one day, Aldo said to me out of the blue, 'They all want to come back to earth, even if it is just for one moment, Mommy.'

'Who are you talking about, Aldo?' I asked.

'The people in hell. All they want is one more chance to receive Jesus into their hearts.'

We finished the rest of the trip without further conversation, only pondering his words that echoed in the silence. I remembered what Jesus said: *'And do not fear those who kill the body but cannot kill the soul. But rather fear Him who is able to destroy both soul and body in hell'* (Matthew 10:28).

het wysheid jou ook gewys
hoe mense het toe gaan
hy wys my waar mense
skreeu want hulle wil so
graag nog n kans he. god
wys my hulle lewe was
nie gegaan aan god nie.
lees Petrus my werk is
om te vertel wat ek gesien
het

> 'Seek the Lord while He may be found.
> Call upon Him while He is near.
> Let the wicked forsake his way, and the unrighteous man
> his thoughts; let him return to the Lord,
> and He will have mercy on him…'
> *- Isaiah 55:6 -*

In this Scripture, God clearly shows us the way through the prophet Isaiah: Not only do we need to call upon the name of the Lord, but we also need to forsake our wicked ways and our unrighteous thoughts. The grace we received through Jesus' blood and His sacrifice is free (not by our works but by God's grace), but it is most definitely not cheap.

Today, I know how important it is to use every opportunity to repent when the Holy Spirit convicts us of sin. The Lord is a holy God coming to fetch a holy, Spirit-Bride. We mustn't quiet the Holy Spirit when He convicts us of sin; we must submit to His ways and seek to follow Him regardless of the cost.

Please be ready when God sends His Son to fetch us.
It is going to be much quicker than you think.
God is coming to fetch His Bride for Jesus.
Please accept Jesus now before it is too late.

Know for certain, there is a hell.
Jesus showed me everything, and believe me,
you don't want to go to hell.
Jesus said those who accept Him will not go to hell.
Heaven consists only of love and
we will live together with Jesus.
Please believe me and accept Jesus quickly.
You can also be His Bride.

Lay down your life for Jesus please!

And now we need to search our hearts, and in all honesty, ask ourselves the most important question there is...

Is my name written in the Lamb's Book of Life?

> 'And I saw the dead, small and great,
> standing before God, and books were opened.
> And another book was opened, which is the Book of Life.
> And the dead were judged according to their works,
> by the things which were written in the books.'
>
> 'And anyone not found written
> in the Book of Life was cast into the lake of fire.'
> *- Revelation 20:12 and 15 -*

In one of his first letters after he awoke from the coma, Aldo wrote a very strange thing: 'Jesus asked me what I did for Him while I was on earth.'

This really surprised me and in my pride I thought to myself, 'What was a twelve-year-old supposed to do except enjoy being twelve years old?'

Today I know better.

Even my youngest son Josh (who is now only eight), should be ready to answer that question. We will *all* need to answer that question and give account of our deeds here on earth.

Please be ready when Jesus comes to fetch His Bride,
like Jesus told me Himself He was coming to do.
I love You Jesus. Teach the people that Jesus loves
them very much. Teach them everyone will stand
before the throne and see his life again.
A lot of them are going to cry and gnash on their teeth,
and then God will be gone and people will want to run away.
Mommy, please warn the people.
Hell is a terrible place.

In another one of our conversations, Aldo told me, 'I saw a lake of fire. The people who were in it, were people who didn't worship Jesus. A lot of them worshiped their own desires, Mommy.'

God knows our hearts, our thoughts, our works, and our motives. The fact that we sit in church every Sunday does not guarantee our entrance through the pearly gates of heaven, because we can be sitting there in body while our hearts are far away, sold out to another god.

When I close my eyes and imagine what that glorious and terrible last day will be like, the first thing I see is all of creation bowing before the King of kings. Every knee shall bow and every tongue shall proclaim Jesus of Nazareth is Lord (see Romans 14:11); but for some, it will be the first time these words are uttered from their lips.

Wysheid se elke tong
ja elke tong sal
belei en elke knieg
sal buig

> *Wisdom says every tongue, yes every tongue,*
> *shall proclaim and every knee shall bow.*

Aldo said that when he stood before the King, his whole life flashed before his eyes. He calls it the 'movie of his life.'

In His presence we will realize the worldly things that were so important to us – things that we built our whole lives around (like striving for success, or riches, or acceptance) – seem like nothing when compared to His glory. We will then realize how fleeting the pleasure was and how much time we wasted on things that were only temporary.

I can only image the questions that will be asked, as we stand in front of His throne: How could I have made a god of these things? Why didn't I spend more time seeking His face and His will for my life? Why didn't I trust Him with my future instead of following my own ways? Why was I so caught up in myself that I missed Him? Why didn't I worship Him in spirit and truth? Why did I waste my life running after things that didn't matter, while He was there all the time? And ultimately: why didn't I love Him and my neighbors, like He told me to?

> *Jesus says what I write is because of God's Spirit and this is how my ministry is starting. God says my work has started.*
> *I want to love God like you love Him, Mommy.*
> *God told me Jesus is on His way and only those who are ready will go with Him. There are a lot who will not go with, because they say they serve God but they are actually worshiping themselves and their own will. God says what will happen to them is the hell.*
> *Hell is a real place.*
> *I saw a lot of people there screaming.*
> *Please warn the people, Mommy, because they don't believe.*
> *What I saw made me cry, Mommy.*
> *I wish Jesus didn't show it to me,*
> *but He said I will tell about everything I saw.*
> *There are so many people.*

In front of the throne we will realize all our fleshly endeavors to please God were only clanging symbols. Let us serve God in spirit and truth! The way to God's heart is through and intimate love relationship, by grace through faith. Our works will then be a testimony of our love for Him.

Jesus gave a stern warning to those who praise Him with their lips but whose hearts are far from Him: *'This people honors Me with their lips, but their heart is far from Me. And in vain they worship Me, teaching as doctrines the commandments of men'* (Mark 7:6-7).

'But God,' we try to justify ourselves, 'we worked so hard. We gave money for outreaches, sold hamburgers at the bazaar, and even sang in the choir!'

The Holy Spirit clearly spoke to me about this and said, 'Send out the warning: Those who claim to know Me, but deny Me by the way they live, must consider the implications of their actions. My Word is My measuring line. Everyone will be judged according to My Word.'

God se Lees
die bybel want weet
jy mense sal geoordeel
word

God says read the Bible, because people will be judged.

'For God so loved the world that He gave
His only begotten Son, that whoever believes
in Him should not perish but have everlasting life.
For God did not send His Son
into the world to condemn the world,
but that the world though Him might be saved.'
- John 3:16-17 -

Listen closely to what Jesus says: 'My blood is freely given to anyone who comes to kneel at My cross. I will not turn anyone away, because the Father has called them to Me. The cross is a place of death and resurrection, where you lose your old life but become reborn – a new creation! It is a place of repentance, but repentance is not words only; repentance is a life of daily dying to self, and living in Christ. Only those who lay down their life, pick up their cross, and follow Me are worthy to be called My disciples. Give Me the place of First Love in your heart, and I will lead you into a life of love. Let My Holy Spirit transform you from the inside out, and become all I have destined You to be. Give Me your best. Give Me your all. Give

Me your life. Not because you are forced to do it, but because you love Me, and you know that I have your best interest at heart. I want you to release what you are holding on to so tightly; and as you open your hands in trust, you will receive so much more.

'Leave the things of the world behind. Stop with the works of the flesh. Seek Me in spirit and truth. Lay down your masks and your hidden sins. I know all there is to know about you – nothing is hidden from before My eyes – and still I love you with so much love that I gave My life for you.

'*If you love Me, keep My commandments,* (John 14:15). My Word and My Spirit must be a part of you. If you don't have My Word and My Spirit, you don't have truth and you won't be able to live according to My will. Let My Spirit engrave My Word on your heart. Don't fill your days with earthly pleasures, and then come home tired saying there wasn't time for Me. If you have time for cake and tea with friends, but you don't have time for Me, there is something seriously wrong with your priorities. Don't you know, I am a jealous God! I am jealous for you. If you have a problem, don't run to the phone first. Run to My throne of grace. Lift your eyes unto the hills and remember where your help comes from.

'And for those who preach My Word: don't you realize you will be judged by a higher standard? (See James 3:1.) That is why it is important to *know* Me, and to live according to My Word. You need to lead the people into the whole truth. Yes, I am the Lamb, but I am also the Lion. Don't seek excuses for sin. Your church, or your ministry, must never become more important than your First Love. Through your love for Me, you will lead by example.

'Yes, My children: Heaven and hell and the day of judgment are realities. Listen to My truth, spoken with so much love, and let the truth set you free (see John 8:32).

'*I am the way, the truth, and the life. No one comes to the Father except through Me'* (John 14:6).

Jesus het vir my gese hy wil nie he mense moet verlore gaan nie. ek moet vir hulle leer dat Jesus lewe. hy is baie lief vir mense weet jy ons sal hierdeur kom. hy sal ons nie los nie. Lief.

> *Jesus told me He doesn't want anybody to be lost.*
> *I must teach them that Jesus is alive. He loves people very*
> *much. We will get through this. He will not leave us.*

'Do not love the world or the things in the world.
If anyone loves the world, the love of the Father is not in him.
For all that is in the world – the lust of the flesh, the lust of the
eyes, and the pride of life – is not of the Father but is of the
world. And the world is passing away and the lust of it;
but he who does the will of God abides forever.'
- 1 John 2:15-17 -

Will we give our First Love, our everything? Will we give Him the best of our time, our resources, our obedience and, especially, our love? To know Him, is to love Him and to love Him is to obey Him.

This message is not soft on the ear, but it is the truth. Yes, there is a heaven. But, yes, there is also a hell. A lot of people know Jesus as the Lamb, but not everyone knows Him as the Lion.

Wysheid het vir my mense gewys wat werklik die hel sal sien weet

hy wil he hulle moet belei
hy wil nie he hulle moet hel
toe gaan nie.

> *Wisdom showed me people that will see hell. Please know He wants them to repent. He doesn't want them to go to hell.*

The day I met God for the first time, the waves that kept on crashing over my spirit were, 'God is love...God is love... God is love...,' This God of love eagerly waits for us to bend the knee, repent, and return to Him. You don't have to end up next to a busy highway, in front of a big red stop sign, like I did. You can make your choice now.

ons sal

hom met verenig word
in die hemel

> *We will be reunited with Him in heaven.*

'See, I have set before you today life and good,
death and evil, in that I command you today
to love the Lord your God,
to walk in His ways and to keep His commandments,
His statutes, and His judgments, that you may live and
multiply; and the Lord your God
will bless you in the land which you go to possess.'
- *Deuteronomy 30:15-16* -

As Moses set it before the Israelites, so Holy Spirit presents the choice to us today.
Let's do it now, not wasting any more time.
Let's kneel before the King and choose life –
a life with Jesus.
Eternal life.

Jesus sê sy eind boodskap
is wees gereed.
Wie nie gereed is nie sal
agter bly.
Wie nie gevul en skoon
gewas is in die bloed
van Jesus nie.
Wie sal wil hel toe gaan?
Dis so baie erg in die hel
wees asb gereed.

Jesus says His message for the endtime is BE READY.
Those who are not ready will stay behind. They are those
who are not filled (with the Holy Spirit) *and washed clean*
(by the blood). *Who will want to go to hell?*
It is very bad in hell.
Please be ready.

A masterpiece in process

Mamma sal wees soos
~~du~~ soos ons God joy
wil hê. Jy sal wysheid
ontvang en gaan Amerika
toe om ~~die~~ boek ~~te~~
publish. God het die
boek en ~~die~~ werkers
geseen dan gaan die
wêreld Hom - loof en
eer. God is in beheer
wys asb God en mense
God is in beheer.
sal jy dit glo asb. God
wys my sy heerlikheid en
sy krag.

> Mommy, you will be what God wants you to be.
> You will receive wisdom, and you will go to America
> to publish the book. God will bless the book
> and those who work with it, so the whole world
> will bless and honor Him. God is in control.

> *Please show the people God is in control. Please believe me.*
> *God shows me His majesty and His power.*

In *A Message From God*, I told the story of how a terrible accident changed our lives for the better. The Lord explained it to me with this simple simile: All the broken pieces of your life are nothing more than the beautiful mosaic of your future.

Through this simile, God once again showed me that life comes down to the choices we make. Some people choose to sit down in the shards of a broken life, and use the pain as an excuse to become bitter and resentful. Others hand the shards to God so that He can reshape their future with His Almighty hand, making it much more beautiful than it was before.

As a family we chose the latter, and today, I boldly proclaim: *'As for me and my house, we will serve the LORD!'* (Joshua 24:15).

Aldo and I grew very close after the accident. We have a special spiritual connection that I can't explain. We were together in the throne room after the accident, and even before he could talk, he would cross his fingers to indicate that we are one. I know he means one in spirit. Even though we are so close, I know he doesn't belong to me – he belongs to God. It is precious to me when he writes that I should give him to God, when I get worried about him.

> *Please, Mommy. You sacrificed me to God.*
> *Please don't take me back.*

Today, we share the same burning passion to tell the world Jesus is alive. Many people ask me why I work so hard. 'Isn't all this traveling wearing you down, Retha? Shouldn't you be taking care of your child when he is so sick?'

I can only answer that I am doing what God has called me to do, and I trust Him completely to take care of all the rest.

In the foyer of my ministry office, I have a beautifully engraved wooden board to remind me of this calling every day.

Every time I walk through the front door and look up, I read:
'Whom shall I send?...Here am I. Send me' (Isaiah 6:8).

> *Work, Mommy, because Jesus is on His way.*
> *God says you trusted Him with everything.*
> *My healing is here. Do you know that I am sorry I hurt you?*

Aldo is my greatest supporter. He is probably also the one who needs me the most, but he encourages me daily to go out and be the hands and feet of Jesus. Sometimes when I return home after an event, He tells me of incidents that took place while I was ministering, even if they happened halfway across the world. He even describes what he sees in the Spirit over a certain area before I go to minister, and that helps me tremendously in my ministry. At the same time, he is also a teenager who can get impatient and then raise his voice (this sounds like yelling, because he can't even talk softly), so please don't think he is perfect! He makes mistakes all the time, but God's grace is always there to pick him up again.

> *You want to show me again how much you love me,*
> *even though I was not nice to you. Sorry, Mommy. I won't do*
> *it again. God says you get hurt very much. Will you please*
> *forgive me? God says you and Daddy will be happy again.*

With all these amazing gifts, you have to keep in mind that Aldo is a seventeen-year-old teenager, still finding his own identity. As with any normal teenager, we have our ups and downs. Tinus and I are responsible for his upbringing and we have to discipline him, just like we do with our other son, Josh.

Tinus and Aldo are also very close. Tinus looks after the kids when I am away. He is in charge of the lunchboxes, homework and swimming practice; and let me tell you, I don't think there are many moms out there who can do it better!

It doesn't matter how difficult or stubborn Aldo might get, Tinus is always there to help. Although Aldo is very strong in the spirit, his soul (mind, will, and emotions) and flesh, still need the discipline and love that work hand in hand, to bring him to maturity in Christ.

Tinus can be very strict with Aldo, but when I see my son's manners and the gentleman he has become, I know it is because of the foundation Tinus has laid. Just because he walks with difficulty, doesn't mean he should slouch through life. Just because he talks slowly, doesn't give him an excuse to greet someone improperly. Tinus is a perfect gentleman, and he is teaching both his sons to follow in his footsteps.

I have an amazing marriage and my husband also loves Jesus with his whole heart. As can be expected, the heartache we went through left wounds in both of us that sometimes lead to arguments. But through it all, we know we are a team. Jesus handpicked Tinus to be my husband, because He knew what was coming long before Aldo was even born. I couldn't have asked for a better person to share this journey with. Tinus is an anchor that holds my feet firmly on the Rock, and his steadfast love gives me the freedom to spread my wings and fly!

When I come home, I don't preach to my husband. I love him, and honor him, and submit to him; for that is the way the Lord intended it to be. I choose to be the least, and hold my tongue in situations where my flesh would like to get the last word in. This did not come easy, but I knew it was part of the *dying to self* process in my life. In every situation, there is an opportunity to become more like Christ. When I choose to submit to God's Word, my flesh automatically has to die. Through this, I can see how both Tinus and I grow in the Lord; just by honoring His principles in our marriage.

Liefde is god en
jy pappa liefhê soos god
jou liefhet.

Love is God, and you must love Daddy like God loves you.

Aldo was extremely sick for most of 2008; and through it all, Tinus never complained. He doesn't resent it when I have to leave to minister, because he knows his role in the house is as much part of the ministry as my standing on stage and preaching.

When I travel, he makes sure the car if full of gas and the GPS is working, that all my books and teaching CDs are packed, and that I have a snack to eat on the road. He treats me like a precious pearl in his crown; and I would never be able to do what God has called me to do without him.

Work for Jesus, because He has called you
especially for Himself.
I am also going to work for Him and have a good wife.
Work and keep on working, because time is running out.
He will give you the strength to do it.

When I come home, Josh tells me they have communion more often when I am away than when I am there; they do it around the dinner table every night. Afterwards, Tinus anoints the boys before they go to bed, and speaks a blessing over them when they go off to school. It is a beautiful sight (and it always brings tears to my eyes) to see Tinus putting his big hands on Aldo's and Josh's heads to bless them for the day ahead. He taught both of them to blow the shofar, and every so often, you will hear the battle cry sounding as the men of my house fight the good fight of faith.

Tinus walks on the water with me, step by step. There is nothing better than to hope together, trust together, love together. There was a time when our marriage was only in survival mode; but as Jesus taught me to love Him, and be intimate with Him, everything changed. The love I received from the King overflowed to my marriage, and today it is stronger than ever before. Now, we set time apart especially for each other. It can be as small as a coffee in town between meetings, or a weekend away just the two of us, but we make sure we spend quality time together. Then I look him in the eyes and tell him how much I love, adore, and appreciate him.

Your marriage is part of your ministry. The way you treat your natural spouse says something of how you treat your heavenly Bridegroom. Marriage should truly be seen as *holy* matrimony; something special, a precious pearl, and a gift of God that needs to be cherished.

God has put a special team together to support me and hold my arms in the air. Tinus is the rock of the family: steadfast, unmoving, a shelter in the storm. My mom is the caretaker and she brings so much love into the house. Whenever I return from an overseas trip, I know there is a home cooked South African meal waiting, and flowers in my bedroom. My dad is always ready to lend a helping hand around the house or with the kids. Both of them flood their grandchildren with love. Miss Patrys looks after Aldo as she would her own son. In those times when I am not around, I know he is in the best possible hands. Kate and Regina, the beautiful ladies working in my house, are part of the family, too. Then there is Aubrey and Master. One works at the office and the other at our house, but after three o'clock they are Aldo's friends. They watch God Channel with him, or play soccer with him, and they even pray with him!

In the office, I have a wonderful team. Judike, my personal assistant, jumped into the deep waters and helped with this book, and I know she is handpicked by God for a time such as this. And dear Maggie patiently handles all the calls and emails and prays for the wounded and hurt with one of the purest hearts I have ever seen. With such an amazing foundation, I can go to wherever God sends me with peace in my heart, because I know He takes care of everything, and that all these precious people are in the palm of His hand. Together we are a team—a team for Jesus!

Because I stand in public ministry, I can sometimes be very hard on myself. I still make a lot of mistakes, and I learn as I go along. The Holy Spirit is always faithful to convict me when I take a misstep. Although I repent when He leads me to, I sometimes hold on to the guilt – struggling to forgive myself. Aldo quickly picks up when I am feeling like this. He then writes:

You are forgiven but you are not accepting it.
Take to heart what God says – He says He is going to use
you to show His power. Become what God asks of you. Holy.

You will receive wisdom from God. You will teach people
about God's Kingdom and His amazing love. Be holy to Jesus.
Mommy, you will teach people about God's love.

'And as you go, preach, saying,
"The kingdom of heaven is at hand."'
- *Matthew 10:7* -

How can I say "No" to a calling such as this? The Lord has paved the way for me to go and build His house, because I know He is faithfully building mine.

'For this One has been counted worthy of more glory
than Moses, inasmuch as He who built the house has
more honor than the house. For every house is built by
someone, but He who built all things is God.'
- *Hebrews 3:3-4* -

I build with stones of forgiveness, mercy, grace, kindness, truth, righteousness, holiness, fear of the Lord, and most importantly, love. Sincere love is to love what is imperfect, perfectly. That is what Jesus did for me: When He picked me up on the side of a busy highway, He didn't condemn me for my past mistakes. No, He stretched out His hand and asked if I wanted to face the future with Him. That is grace.

And His mercies are new every morning! I hold on to this truth, because every morning when I wake up, I am aware of how desperately dependent I am on Him.

> *God cannot lie. You want to protect me but you can't.*
> *Mommy, I will be as I always was. Please believe God.*
> *He says you will experience it yourself.*
> *Do you know, Mommy, that you are very special?*
> *There are not many people who would*
> *have gone on believing. Thank you, Mommy.*

'But without faith it is impossible to please Him,
for he who comes to God must believe that He is, and
that He is a rewarder of those who diligently seek Him.'
- Hebrews 11:6 -

The day I met God, I realized: He is truly alive! Thereafter it wasn't difficult for me to have faith. Today, faith is to me something completely different from what most other people think it is. Faith is to be aware of the precious, sweet, presence of God in me. Jesus Christ, the Word of God, in me! I now believe with the God-type of faith. That is also why I will never give up hope, because the power is not from myself, but Jesus Christ is my hope of glory! If Jesus saw the potential, then it must be attainable.

I will never give up on Aldo.
I will never give up on God's promises.
I will never give up on Jesus.
Christ in me – my hope of glory!
Selah.

Tinus and Retha

Tinus — The hardest race of our lives

Liewe Pappa
Jesus se Jy het
hom alles gegee
hy se Jy sal nie
teleurgestel word nie
hy se hy hou jou
vas werk meneer hy
gaan alles verander hy
voor jou oe. hy gaan
kir jou jou begeerte
van jou hart gee. Wys
heid se Jy wyn geoffer
wysheid se Jy sal
vinnig god se genade
hy wil jou help wys
my hoe Jy wysheid
het wysheid wys jou

Dear Daddy,
Jesus said you gave Him everything.
He says you will not be disappointed.
He says He is holding you tightly. Work, Mister.
He is going to change everything in front of your eyes.
He is going to give you the desire of your heart.
Wisdom says you have offered drinking wine to Him.

> *Wisdom says you will experience the grace of God.*
> *He wants to help you.*
> *He shows me that you have Wisdom.*

No one could have prepared me for the heartache, pain, and uncertainty of what the future may hold, when tragedy hit. When I stood in front of my son's hospital bed (whose dreams I dreamt for him), and there was no telling if he would live through the night, my entire life crumbled.

Suddenly, all the problems I ever faced before in my life, combined, seemed totally irrelevant compared to what I was facing now.

I didn't know if I wanted to cry, yell, or just lie down and die. The thoughts of Aldo's little brother Josh (2), and Retha, who also shared my pain, pulled me back to reality. My sense of responsibility kept me going for the time being – but the pain didn't go away.

Everyone that visited us in the hospital said it was absolutely normal to blame yourself, and even blame God, in these types of traumatic situations.

The latter wasn't an option to us. Although we didn't have an idyllic relationship with God at that time in our life, our family knew where our strength and help would come from as we stood beside the wreckage on the side of a national highway.

Three days after the accident, I was compelled by necessity to return to my office. Totally unsure of what the future might hold, I called all my employees into the office and told them, 'From today, this business belongs to God. We will come together every Monday morning to dedicate each worker, his family, and every client to God.' Twenty-five blank expressions stared back at me, trying to process the dramatic change in their boss. But everyone bowed their heads in prayer, in agreement.

While standing next to Aldo's bed, all the memories of the good times we shared passed through my mind. I remembered our first bicycle race when he was only eight years old. When we hit the first steep uphill climb, I put my hand on his back and started pushing him up the hill. On our way to the top, we passed a lot of his local heroes or friends who got off their bikes to walk the rest of the way, because the hill was so steep. Once we got to the top, a surprised Aldo looked down the hill and then back at me and said, 'Daddy, we can win this race if we work together!'

Where I stood in front of his hospital bed, with tears streaming down my face, I realized we were at the start of the hardest race of our lives. Not knowing if he could hear me, I bent down and whispered in his ear, 'Aldo, we can win this race if we work together.'

The next three months was one big juggling act between taking care of Josh, making ends meet at the business, and hospital visiting hours.

When his condition did not improve after those initial three months (and because the doctors could do nothing more for him), we made the best decision we could have possibly made, and we took him home to look after him ourselves.

Now we had the added responsibility of keeping our twelve-year-old son, who was connected to a feeding-tube, alive. After the first few nights without any sleep, we realized we were definitely going to need some help. Thereafter, our house had a constant flow of nursing personnel and therapists coming in and out. The toughest part of managing all of them was convincing them of what we knew to be true: *That God was in control!*

The worst part was to see our child completely dependent on the help of strangers. Every time, I blamed myself for the predicament our family found ourselves in. I decided I had one of two options: the easy way out would be to feel sorry for myself and hope everyone else would do the same, *or* I could pick myself up from the ground, put my trust in God, and face the future with hope.

In the process, our entire family started walking a very narrow road with God. Our hope was placed fully in Him for everything we needed, for every step of Aldo's healing and even the funds to finance the road — and we have never been disappointed. Things may not have happened as quickly as we wanted them to, but every time, at the right time, we received what we needed.

Most of my friends quickly disappeared, because this new road we were on was just too strange for them. But God sent new people to take their place. I will always be thankful for each of them, but I don't expect anybody to understand our pain.

As Aldo started growing older, my faith was challenged more and more. When he started writing prophetically, it was totally strange and new to me. The letters testified of a new Aldo – not at all like the twelve-year-old boy I knew before the accident. It took me a while to realize there is a distinct difference between body, soul, and spirit.

Even after Retha publicly started ministering about our testimony, it was hard for me to come to terms with the new direction in which our lives were heading. It felt as if our pain, that was so private and still very raw, was being put on display for the world to see. Only after I read some of the e-mails people sent to Retha, telling of how our testimony changed their lives, did I realize that God was using our testimony for His glory. By wanting to keep it to myself, I was standing in the way of His divine master plan.

For the first eighteen months, Aldo was either in his bed or in his wheelchair. He lost a lot of weight, which made it easy for me to carry him around. We started exercising with him. In the mornings we did it by ourselves, and in the afternoons the physical therapists were there to help. It took three people to get him to walk two steps. Retha's knees were permanently full of scratch marks because of these training sessions.

Later, we upgraded to a practice bicycle in our living room. We would turn his feet with our hands to get his brain to remember the pathways of physical movement. As I turned his feet, pedal-stroke for pedal-stroke, I felt like a steam engine determinately pushing my way forward. I refused to listen to any negative commentary from the outside world. Walking a road of faith means you stand with one foot on the edge of a disaster, and the other foot on the edge of a miracle. You cannot afford to lose your focus on Jesus.

On the thirty-first of December, only six months after the accident, our Aldo was sitting in a wheelchair. A year before, we had run a ten-kilometer fun run around Sea Point in Cape Town (a race held in commemoration of athletes who had died during practice or while participating in races). On this December morning, after the accident, we decided to run the race again, and Aldo was going with us! We pushed him in his wheelchair the entire ten kilometers. At the finish line, there was a crowd waiting to receive us with applause. Then and there, we decided to make Aldo a part of our everyday lives, even if it was sometimes uncomfortable and we had to endure the curious stares of onlookers.

After training Aldo for six months on the practice bicycle in our living room, father and son started practicing with a tandem bicycle. We would clip his feet to the pedals, fasten his hands with bandages to the handle bar, and I would be responsible for the navigation. At first we didn't get very far; but later, as we became stronger and stronger, I entered us in a forty kilometer bike race. I told Aldo that morning, while looking at the overcast sky, that if it was going to rain we weren't going to race. He earnestly started praying for the rain to stay away and five minutes later the raindrops ceased, and we were off! After a few grueling hours, it was one of the happiest moments of my life when the two of us crossed over the finish line.

The path since then has not been easy (it still isn't), but I now know God is more interested in my character than my comfort.

To be honest, there were many days when I longingly remembered my out-of-breath, red-faced boy who returned from rugby practice and left his bicycle in the driveway, and his backpack in the hall; and then fell down on the couch with a cool drink in hand.

But now, when I come home and find him in the living room where he is sitting with his Bible, or just kneeling with arms outstretched, praying for hours and calling on God, all the longing disappears and I am the proudest dad on earth.

Aldo and Tinus

Josh –
The next generation

Ek is baie baie lief vir Jesus.

Hy het my boetie se lewe gered.

Jesus het my gevang toe ek uit die kar geval

het met die ongeluk.

Jesus het een nag kom hallo sê, Hy het
vir my gewaai. Hy het geklop aan my
deur van my hart. Ek en Heilige Gees is
Dit was donker in die gang toe ek my nagklere gaan vriende.
toe begin die engel vir my sing.

Ek hou van om vir Jesus te sing. Ek wil
baie graag eendag 'n plaas he en soos oom
Angus praat vir Jesus

Ek is baie bly Aldo is gesond
Ek help altyd Aldo onthou dat hy
gan eendag vir Jesus praat liefde
Josh

178

> *I love Jesus very much. He saved my brother's life. Jesus caught me when I fell out of the car at the accident. Jesus came to say hello to me one night, and He waved at me. He knocked at the door of my heart. Holy Spirit and I are friends. It was dark one night when I went to fetch my pajamas and then the angels started singing to me. I like to sing for Jesus. I would really like to have a farm one day and preach about Jesus like Uncle Angus. I am very happy Aldo is healthy. I always remind Aldo that He is going to preach for Jesus one day. Love, Josh*

Josh is part of a new generation – the Benjamin generation.

When I look at him, I can see how the grace of God covers every step of his life. He excels in everything he puts his hands to. He is brought up in a house where everything is about the King. We don't just talk the talk, but we walk the walk – the walk of faith!

While I was ministering in America, Tinus being at home with the boys, took them for a movie and a milkshake over the weekend. While they were waiting for their order to arrive, a young boy came up to Josh and invited him to play outside. After a little while, Josh came back and quietly slipped in next to Tinus.

Curious, Tinus asked him, 'What happened, Josh? Don't you want to play with your new friend anymore?'
In between milkshake sips, he answered, 'No, Daddy, he wanted to play a game where he *abracadabra's* me into a dog, and Mommy taught me not to sit with fools. So I left.'

I taught Aldo and Josh this truth from Psalm 1:1-2: 'Blessed is the man who walks not in the counsel of the ungodly, nor stands in the paths of sinners, nor sits in the seat of the scornful; but his delight is in the law of the LORD.' Josh knows we don't just listen to the Word of God in our house, we need to live it!

I especially like to pray this Scripture over my family:

'But He said to me, My grace (My favor and loving-kindness and mercy) is enough for you [sufficient against any danger and enables you to bear the trouble manfully]; for My strength and power are made perfect (fulfilled and completed) and show themselves most effective in [your] weaknesses. Therefore, I will all the more gladly glory in my weaknesses and infirmities, that the strength and power of Christ (the Messiah) may rest **(yes, may pitch a tent over and dwell)** *upon me!'*
(2 Corinthians 12:9 AMP).

One afternoon Josh came into our room with a small camping tent under his arm. He wanted to play 'tent-tent' with me. After he set it up, I climbed in with him. As we sat inside, I realized that all I could see was tent, all I could smell was tent, and all I was aware of was tent. The outside world seemed galaxies away and I felt so safe. This is exactly what God's grace does for us – it pitches a tent of safety and security over us, a secret place where we can hide.

Josh's tent was very small, and we had to lie close to each other in order to fit in. I could feel Josh's heartbeat as I tickled his back. We were so close to each other that I only had to whisper, 'Joshie, I love you,' and softly, he answered back, 'I love you too, Mommy.'

The next day, he wanted to play 'tent-tent' again. This time, he ran to my study and fetched my Jewish prayer shawl (called a *tallit*), and used it as his canopy. He threw the tallit over himself, and the next moment, he started speaking in a heavenly language. He jumped up and babbled on in this new language for a few seconds more. Then he looked at me ever so surprised, and said in Afrikaans, 'Mommy, I spoke to Jesus! But it was in His language because we were in His tent, right?'

All I could do was smile at his childlike faith. The Word of God says all of us have to become like children to enter the Kingdom of God (see Matthew 18:3). We must also start believing like first-graders that nothing is impossible for God!

There were so many nights when we used to sit up until long past midnight with Aldo because of his epilepsy. (I am so thankful those sleepless nights are over! Aldo hasn't suffered an attack in months, and I believe he never will again.) Whenever I looked at Josh during those sessions, he would be sitting with his arms outstretched towards Aldo, praying fervently for his brother. Josh was a real faith warrior. He amazed me, because he never gave up. He kept on praying, no matter how tired he was.

As a family, the four of us sometimes kneel in a circle to pray. Josh calls this our popcorn prayer. Everyone gets a turn, and the first one who wants to 'pop' can pray.

Curious, I asked, 'Josh, how will we know who pops first?'

'That's easy, Mom,' he replied. 'Holy Spirit's fire makes people pop. You can't do it out of yourself. Only when His fire makes you warm, are you allowed to pray.'

With this easy-to-understand example, I realized we must wait on Holy Spirit to lead us in prayer. Then when we 'pop,' our words are a sweet-smelling aroma to the King. Josh learned this amazing 'popcorn prayer' from his first-grade teacher. I praise God for raising up teachers who mentor our children in the ways of God, and not only that 1 + 1 = 2.

Whenever I am home over the weekend, we celebrate the Jewish *Shabbat* dinner on Friday nights. This is not to bind us again to the Law, but rather to bind us together in love. We use this opportunity to celebrate Christ in our lives. During the week, I look forward to Friday nights with great joy and anticipation. When I am not in town, I even make special arrangements to change my flight details so I can be in time for Shabbat dinner. As we sit around the table as a family, we talk about the goodness of God that followed us during the week; and I listen to my children's stories of how they served others. It is very important to me that they know the Bride of Christ should serve, not just sit back and receive.

According to the Jewish tradition, the woman of the house plays a very important role throughout the dinner. She prepares the feast. The head of the house, her husband, honors his wife by buying her a bouquet of flowers. When I am home, my faithful Tinus always buys me flowers – and through the flowers he shows his appreciation and his love. Whenever I am away, he sends me my 'flowers' in a text message, telling me what a special and irreplaceable part of the family I am. These messages are like roses that will never wilt!

The Shabbat dinner begins with me lighting the candles, signifying that Jesus is the Light of the world. Through this prophetic act, we also invite God to sit at the place of highest honor at our table. Then we read Scriptures from the Word of God, and Tinus blesses each member of our family. My husband places his big hands on each of my sons' heads and pronounces a blessing over them individually. I can never seem to hold back the tears when I see this beautiful picture!

One night, Tinus got so carried away pronouncing blessings over Josh that his head drooped to his plate while his dad went on and on. After Tinus finally said 'Amen,' Josh looked up and said, 'No, Daddy. You should keep going. Please bless me more!'

As a family, we build our lives on the blessings of God. Parents can either bless or curse their children through their words. Many of the next generation have fallen into rebellion because of careless words spoken over them. Our words will either build or break.

After eating, we share communion.

One night after communion, Josh asked, 'Can we wash Jesus' feet tonight?'

A bit unsure of how to do this, I asked, 'And how are we going to do that, Joshie?'

He jumped up and fetched my most expensive perfume, a beautiful white towel, and a silver bowl. Then he sat down cross-legged in the middle of our living room carpet.

'Come on guys. Come sit with me.'

Once we were all sitting cross-legged with him, around the bowl now filled with hot water, Josh lifted his hands in the air and invited Jesus into our circle. Quietly, we all waited for Jesus to show up. A few moments passed and then we were all crying, because the presence of our Lord was so tangibly with us. We mustn't think if we invite Jesus, He won't show up. I believe, with the eyes of our heart, all of us saw Jesus' pierced feet through our tears. I know I did.

Many times I am reminded that our situation in the natural is not as perfect as those of most other families, but what I experience in the Spirit with them is more than perfect to me!

Josh loves to sing. While we were driving down to the Cape for our December holiday, worship music played continually in the car. His hands were lifted high most of the time as he sang to Jesus with all of his heart. The rest of the family kept on chatting through all of his singing, but only until he silenced us. 'Hey, guys, where is your fear of God? Can't you see I am worshiping the King here!' From this, I could see that his level of intimacy with Jesus, at age eight, is something I only discovered at age forty.

On Sunday afternoons, Josh packs his backpack with grape juice, some crackers, and an extra plastic bowl for his dog, Moya. Moya is our spaniel and one of Josh's best friends. He then hops on his bicycle and rides until he finds his favorite spot: a place hidden near an old tree. There, he and Moya will have communion with Jesus.

Sometimes if it gets late and Josh hasn't come home yet, we will go looking for him. We always find him in the same place. His excuse is that he had to wait for the sun to set, because Jesus enjoys watching the sunset with him.

When we are at home and the sun is setting, my boys run to the balcony, put their arms in the air, and say, 'Thank You, Jesus, for another wonderful day!' Even if the day wasn't all that great, they always say thank you.

Josh is the sunshine in our house. I no longer want to boast about my children's school reports or sport achievements. To know that they love God with all their hearts makes me the happiest mom on earth.

When I look at our two sons, I know each one has a unique calling and God-given destiny. I thank God that He loaned them to me for my time here on earth. Both of them belong to God and God alone.

Josh and Moya

Aldo and Josh

PART 2:

Walking
in the Spirit

Empty your hands

Jesus, ek gaan weer word
wat ek was. God gaan woord
gee en geloof sal my
weer bring en wys wat my
doel is op aarde.
Ek is hier om mense
te vertel dat Jesus leef
mamma moet my asb.
asb. offer aan Jesus.

Mamma moet nie
bekommerd wees oor my
genesing nie. God is in beheer.

Ek sal gesond word voor
julle of ook gaan ek oor
tv wees glo net God sal
dit doen. God sal jou
weer genade gee vir
die pad vorentoe. Ons gaan
God beleef soos met die ongeluk.

> *Jesus says I am going to be the same as I was before the*
> *accident. God is going to give the word, and through faith,*
> *I will know what my purpose is on earth.*
> *I am here to tell people Jesus is alive.*
> *Mommy, you must please offer me to Jesus.*
> *Mommy, you should not be worried*
> *about my healing at all. God is in control.*
> *I will be healed right in front of your eyes and*
> *I will testify on television. Just believe that God will do this.*
> *God will give you grace for the road that lies ahead.*
> *We will experience God like we did at the accident.*

To serve God, means total surrender. We raise the white flag and give the King of kings the throne of First Love in our hearts. Not only that, but we lay down our dreams, desires, and accomplishments; also our weaknesses, and shortcomings. When we come to God, we need to come with our whole heart, not only parts thereof – He wants us to lay down everything. God's grace allows us to lay down the good and the bad. We don't have to be ashamed of our weakness; we must bring it before God. If we attempt to hold back some things, hoping to sort it out in our own strength, we take a yoke upon ourselves that will quickly become too heavy to carry. Completely surrendered and totally dependent on God is the best place to be, but it requires trust.

One afternoon, I was walking up the steps to my house, grocery packages hanging from every finger. On the way to the kitchen, someone interrupted me. The longer we stood chatting in the hallway, the heavier the packages became in my hands, until I couldn't hold them any longer. My hands were hurting and could feel the plastic bags cutting into my fingers. I hastily excused myself and ran to put the packages down on the kitchen table. In the same way, things that we hold on to in life leave scars if we don't let go.

Later, Holy Spirit spoke to me regarding the incident and said, 'Retha, when you come to Jesus, immediately put down all your packages at the cross. Repent that the "selfish I" wanted to take control again. Let the blood wash you clean, and give your burdens to Him.'

While I was speaking to Holy Spirit about my own heavy packages, He showed me some things that make our life-bags very heavy — things that we need to put down at the cross. 'Do you really mean I need to lay down everything at Your feet Lord — from my greatest concern to the smallest detail of my life?'

'Remember, My child,' He answered softly, 'nothing is too big or too small for Me. I care for everything about you.'

Holy Spirit taught me what cross-time at Jesus' feet is: to lay down the burdens, to repent and be washed clean, and then to put up our empty hands as high as we can, and praise Him!

When we go into God's presence with murmuring and complaining, and then leave still murmuring and complaining, we haven't truly prayed. Prayer is not a monologue! Prayer is a place where we lay down our heavy burdens and then Jesus gives us His soft yoke to take up. With new hope and a song of praise, we can then stand up from where we knelt and look life (and every difficult situation) in the eye. In true prayer God also has opportunity to let His heartbeat be heard. God's desire is for intimacy, not superficial chatter.

Wie met God 'n pad stap sal beleef dat God getrou is. en die wat op Hom wag kry nuwe krag.

> *Those who walk a road with God will come to know that God is faithful. Those who wait on God will receive new strength.*

> 'Therefore humble yourselves under the mighty hand of God,
> that He may exalt you in due time,
> casting all your cares upon Him, for He cares for you.'
> *- 1 Peter 5:6-7 -*

I emptied my hands at the cross. I laid down my children, my marriage, my finances, my dreams, my business, my friends and family — literally everything that makes me who I am – including my weaknesses. I entrusted the King with my entire life. Why? Because I understood His character. He can carry what I can't. Even my self-centeredness and shortcomings is now at the foot of the cross. I could immediately feel the difference – there was peace in my heart.

God can only change what He has in His hands. That is why it is so important not to hold anything back. Every morning I place my spirit, Tinus' and each of our children's spirits, in the palm of God's hand, just like Psalm 31:5 says: *'Into Your hand I commit my spirit....'*

> *Do you want to know?*
> *God will never leave you nor forsake you.*
> *Will you be like Samuel's mother and offer me to God again?*

The principles of the kingdom of God are in so many aspects directly opposite from the principles of the kingdom of this world. The world teaches us to strive in order to succeed. People struggle with their weaknesses and think if they can only exercise more self-control, they will be better Christians. But God says when we are weak then we are strong, because His power is made perfect in weakness (see 2 Corinthians 12:9). When we come to Him in our brokenness, desperate in our dependence on Him, His strength will heal our weakness.

The world teaches the ten-step program to victory, but God says, 'No, My child. There is only one step. Let the sinner die to himself and be raised in Christ.' In my eyes, that step is when we bend our knees before the Living God. Something significant happens in the spiritual realm when we get down on our knees.

Jesus, our perfect example, showed us the way:

> For though He was crucified in weakness,
> yet He goes on living by the power of God.
> *- 2 Corinthians 13:4 AMP -*

So too we will go on living by the power of God if our weakness is crucified with Jesus. I have found this victory every time I kneel in my bathroom (my favorite place of prayer in my house). There, on the thick carpet, next to the bath I have emptied my hands time after time. My bathroom has become my secret hiding place.

The emptier our hands become, the easier it is to raise our arms in worship. When I pray for people, and I ask them to lift their hands to the King, some hesitate. The reason might be that their hands are too heavy — full of worries, the "selfish I," and pride. The things they hold on to make it difficult to find a reason to lift their hands in worship.

There are days when Aldo seems so weak and sick that I can feel worry and fear nudging at me to take matters back into my own hands. I have come to recognize worry as an archenemy – it steals my joy and wounds my faith. Worry means I take my eyes off Jesus and focus on my problem. Always remember, God did not give us *'a spirit of fear, but of power and of love and of a sound mind'* (2 Timothy 1:7).

Every time fear tries to overpower me, I fall on my face and call out to Jesus, 'Jesus, I surrender this situation to You again, Lord! In Your hands I place my weakness.' This absolute dependency on Jesus is the antidote to worry and fear. On my knees, I then boldly go to the throne of grace, to receive my grace and mercy in a time of need (see Hebrews 4:16).

We mustn't think that when a problem crosses our path, that we can sit back and relax while God sorts it out for us. No, we must go to the throne of grace, in order to receive grace and mercy. God stands ready and willing to extend grace, but we need to go to His throne. There in the Kingdom of light we will find everything we need. It is presumptuous to think that God will automatically move every time we have a need – we also have a role to play. God is moved by faith. The moment God sees faith, He takes action. The Bible promises that if we draw near to God, He will draw near to us (see James 4:8), but we must take the first step.

Aldo can discern in the Spirit when I try to take matters into my own hands, when I become worried. A letter will follow soon afterwards: 'Please, Mommy. Give me to Jesus.'

Jesus sal my gesond maak en
ek sal Hom glo en vertrou
Jy sal my soos Abrahcaham
en Isak offer

> *Jesus will heal me, and I will trust and believe Him.*
> *You will offer me to God as Abraham offered Isaac.*
> *God will touch me. Work together with God,*
> *and know I will do so, too.*

Every day I realize more and more that Aldo doesn't belong to me. The package containing his healing is too heavy for me to carry. The only thing that keeps me standing is to know that Jesus is in control.

Many people ask me how I can continue believing even after all this time. The answer to that is easy – I stand on the Rock. Nothing can shake me, not even time. I trust in God's power, not in my own strength. Aldo's healing is not my responsibility; Jesus will take care of it. All I have to do is keep on trusting Him. We can only walk by faith if we understand

God's character and if we know that Jesus Christ lives in us, and we in Him. The more intimately we know Him, the more we will trust Him. I have never met a child who knows and loves his father, and then is scared to jump when Daddy stands waiting with open arms. Children jump, no matter how high the wall is! It is so sad that God's children say to Him: 'I'll rather try and climb down from this high wall myself – even if it hurts me – before I trust You, and jump into Your arms.'

Jesus is the same yesterday, today and forever (see Heb. 13:8). It is He who made the blind see and the lame walk – it is also He who will finish what He started in Aldo. But the *'two-minute-noodle'* society that we live in today insists that everything should be quick and easy. That is why we become impatient when we wait on God. God uses the waiting period to form wisdom, knowledge, spiritual maturity, patience (and above all), godly character in us. I have learned that what God forms *in* me during the waiting period is usually more precious than what I waited for.

Late one night I was on my face before God again, laying down the worry and fear that so easily tries to find a foothold in my heart, when Aldo walked in. 'What is wrong, Mommy?' he asked.

I answered him through my tears, 'All is well, Aldo. I am just surrendering you to Jesus again.'

> *Did you feel God's presence in your room?*
> *He was there with you.*
> *Will you always offer me to God?*

Jesus invites us to walk alongside Him on the road of the unknown – we don't need to know what lies around the next bend, we only need to trust Him:

> 'Come to Me, all you who labor and are heavy laden, and I will give you rest. Take My yoke upon you and learn from Me, for I am gentle and lowly in heart,

and you will find rest for your souls.
For My yoke is easy and My burden is light.'
- Matthew 11:28-30 -

Jesus wants us to lay everything down and take up His yoke. As long as we hold on to our heavy burdens, He can't do anything. Once everything is at His feet, we will no longer be praying: 'Please bless my plans, Lord!', but we will pray: 'Thank You, Lord, that I can trust You with everything!' Because we know and love Him, we won't find it difficult to trust Him.

When our hands are empty, worry and fear can't come near us, because *we* are not in control, Jesus is. The peace that transcends all understanding is the exclusive privilege of those who trust Him (see Philippians 4:7).

Let's go boldly to the throne of grace, with empty hands lifted high into the air as we praise Him.

Jesus wys my 'n riet
in 'n vlei. moses wat God
se vriend was
God se Hy wil jou
vriend wees. God se Hy
Luister na ons wense
en God Gaan my self
Gesond maak wie my
weggooi sal verlore wees.
Laat God toe om deur jou
te praat mamma. Hy gaan
jou gebruik. Wees oop vir God
mamma Hy sal nie 'n Geknakte riet
breek nie -

Jesus shows me a reed in a valley. Moses was God's friend. God says He wants to be your friend, too. God says He listens to the desires of our hearts and God Himself will heal me. Let God speak through you, Mommy. He will use you. Be open to God, Mommy. God says He won't break a bruised reed.

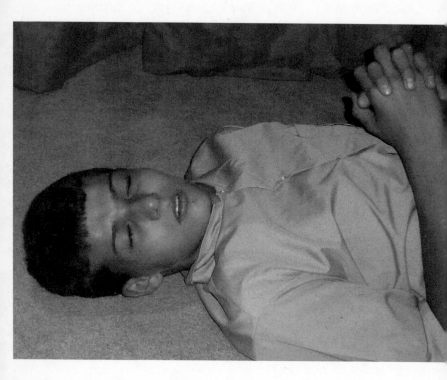

He wants your life

Wysheid se elke tong
ja elke tong sal
belei en elke knieg
sal buig en en my
vrou sal God dien.
Weet jy ek sal eendag
weer my eie kar he
wysheid se weet
het ek en wysheid
werk saam. ag ek gaan
mev baie mis wanneer
sy weer weg gaan. God
se jy en ek weet wat
gaan nou gebeur. Geloof
my mamma ek wens my
herstel kom gou want
ek het so baie om te
vertel. weet jy wat ek
weet verseker ek sal gesond
wees. God se ons doen-
wat hy se. ek gaan-
nou slaap en dan-
na Jesus toe.
elke nag gaan
ek.

> *Wisdom says every tongue will proclaim and every knee*
> *will bow, and my wife and me will serve God.*
> *Do you know that I will have my own car one day?*
> *Wisdom says you must know that Wisdom and I work to-*
> *gether. I am going to miss you a lot when you go away again,*
> *Ma'am. God says that you and I both know what is going to*
> *happen. Faith, Mommy. I wish my recovery will come quickly*
> *because I have so much to tell. I know for certain*
> *that I will be healed. God says we are doing as He instructed.*
> *I want to sleep now and go to Jesus.*
> *I go to Him every night.*

God knew about your life before you were born. He created you for a purpose. That godly calling on your life, to be *one* with Him, is the deepest desire of every human heart – even if not everyone admits it.

He wants to transform each of His sons and daughters into His likeness and engrave His character on our hearts. He wants to fill us with Himself and release His power *in* us, so it can flow *through* us, to reach those who are not yet one with Him.

Only in oneness with Him will we be able to accomplish what we were created for; and only when we walk in our divine destiny, will we find true peace and contentment. There is nothing more fulfilling than knowing your life is sold out to God!

To get to that place of *oneness*, there is a price. That price is nothing more, and nothing less, than your life.

> *Jesus was here last night, and He says you were very tired.*
> *He came to give you wisdom.*
> *You want to please Him.*
> *He wants your life. Listen to His voice.*
> *My job is to pray for people and they will live again.*

> *God wants to show us His Word is power.*
> *I saw the throne room again.*

When I teach on this subject, I frequently get asked questions like: 'Retha, does that mean I have to resign my job and start working in full-time ministry?'

No, not your job, but your *life*. Your life includes everything about you, from the moment you wake up in the morning to the moment you lay down again, and everything in between. God wants it all. He wants to be the center of everything.

God desires to be your first love. To put it simply: He doesn't want anything to be more important than Him. Not your career, money, sports, or even your children. We need to ask the Holy Spirit to show us our hearts; and then make sure that God is our deepest love and highest priority.

After searching in his own heart, the apostle Paul said:

> 'I have been crucified with Christ;
> it is no longer I who live, but Christ lives in me,
> and the life which I now live in the flesh
> I live by faith in the Son of God,
> who loved me and gave Himself for me.'
> - *Galatians 2:20* -

Can we say the same?

Because if we have truly died to ourselves, we will no longer fight to live a selfish life, but everything we encounter (good or bad), will be an opportunity to become more like Christ. There is no other way to put the old self to death except by being crucified with Christ. There are no shortcuts. Only if we die with Him, can we be resurrected with Him – and become reborn (new creations) in the Kingdom of God.

> 'Jesus answered and said to him, "Most assuredly, I say to you, unless one is born again, he cannot see the kingdom of God."'
> - *John 3:3* -

Many people confuse rebirth with church membership. Rebirth doesn't come from an institution; rebirth only takes place when we make a life-changing decision: the day when we come to the end of ourselves, and hand over to Jesus. (If our lives don't testify of being surrendered to Him, it wasn't rebirth.) We then change from being flesh-driven to being Spirit-driven, and we start walking on the road of holiness. The reality is that God requires complete surrender, because a lukewarm Christian will definitely be spewed out (see Revelation 3:15-16).

Jesus says that we will see Him in heaven.
I have seen Him in heaven as I see Him when He comes to me at night and talks to me about people that still need to be saved. He says that He requires everybody to be reborn.
Mommy, do you know that Jesus says those who give Him the honor He deserves and obey Him are His children?
He wants our lives.

Unfortunately, God sometimes needs to put up a big, red, stop sign, before we change direction. When we end up here, there is no Plan B. I have seen how people end up before the stop sign and then still argue with God, and blame Him for the situation. Please don't do that! It wastes precious time. Let us give over to God so that He can show us the way going forward.

> 'Now, therefore,' says the LORD,
> 'turn to Me with all your heart,
> with fasting, with weeping and with mourning.'
> So rend your heart and not your garments;
> return to the LORD your God,
> for He is gracious and merciful, slow to anger,
> and of great kindness; and He relents from doing harm.'
> *- Joel 2:12-13 -*

This place of surrender is very difficult for some, because it means we come face to face with our vulnerability and weakness. The world teaches us: Take control! And so, we hold on to the reins of our life with everything we have, and every now and again we look over our shoulder and say: 'Bless this ride, Lord Jesus!' God wants us to hand over the reins of our life and trust Him.

When I came to this place of total surrender, and handed my reins to God, He picked me up in His awesome love and put me down at the foot of the cross of Jesus. This is where rebirth takes place – when we come to understand with our heart (not only with your mind and from Sunday school stories), what Jesus did for us on the cross. This understanding of the heart (revelation knowledge) is something no one can steal away, because the Holy Spirit engraves it eternally on our hearts. What the Holy Spirit engraves, should rule over the opinion of man, religious man-made ideas, and dogma.

ek weet Jesus leef en hy het vir my weer herinner wat hy aan die kruis gedoen het. Weet jy Jesus is getrou hy sal klaar maak wat hy begin het.

> *I know Jesus lives, and He has reminded me of what He did on the cross. Do you know Jesus is faithful? He will complete what He started.*

Dying to self is to become desperately dependent on God. In every decision and action we have to honor Him. This means we can no longer rely on our human wisdom or fleshly strength. Now, God makes the decisions, and all we have to do is obey and trust. Jesus said: *'I am the vine. You are the branches. He who abides in Me, and I in him, bears much fruit;* **for without Me you can do nothing'** (John 15:5). To die to self is a choice we need to make every day. Paul made this principle so simple when he said: *'I die daily'* (1 Corinthians 15:31).

Jesus not only came to save us from our sins, but also to save us from ourselves and our corrupted human nature. The moment we stop living for ourselves, and instead live only to please Christ, our lives will change dramatically.

The Lord explained it to me this way with a picture: With my spiritual eyes I saw a cup almost filled to the brim with dirty water. There was no room for anything else in this cup, because the stale, stinking water was taking up all the space. I then saw the cup tilting to the one side, and the water flowing out, little by little. The more the cup tilted, the more water flowed out, and the emptier the cup became. The cup could now be filled with living water! Every time we deny our selfish desires to become more like Christ, we *die to self*, and God can fill us up with living water.

At rebirth, God awakens your spirit man. God is Spirit, and when He speaks, He speaks to your spirit. Only when your spirit is alive in Him, will you be able to do what He has called you to do, because only then will you be able to hear what that divine destiny is.

Our purpose on earth is first of all to love the Lord our God, with all our heart, mind, and strength, and then to love our neighbors as ourselves (see Mark 12:30-31). This means our divine destiny is to become like Jesus! When we are one with Jesus, we will become like Jesus, and then do the works He did. All of this is only possible if we know Him, love Him, follow Him, and obey Him.

Do you know, Mommy, I love Jesus because He died for me?
Know wisdom comes from God. Please believe me.

> *You have God's power in you. You must pray for people.*
> *God wants to touch them.*

'If you abide in Me, and My words abide in you,
you will ask what you desire, and it shall be done for you.

By this My Father is glorified, that you bear much fruit,
so you will be My disciples.
As the Father loved Me, I also have loved you;
abide in My love. If you keep My commandments,
you will abide in My love, just as I have
kept My Father's commandments and abide in His love.

These things I have spoken to you,
that My joy may remain in you, and that your joy may be full.
This is My commandment that you love one another
as I have loved you.'
- John 15:7 -

Often, more times than I can count, I have heard Holy Spirit saying to my heart: 'Remember, Retha – the miracle's name is love!'

Jesus loved us to the fullest degree, and that was the cross. Jesus laid down His life because of love. If we love as Jesus taught us through His example to love, then we will abide in Him. And when we walk in selfless love, God knows He can trust us with spiritual authority and power – because we will be like Jesus, and our requests will be in line with His will. Just like Paul, we will then say: *'I count all things loss for the excellence of the knowledge of Christ Jesus my Lord, for whom I have suffered the loss of all things, and count them as rubbish that I may gain Christ'* (Philippians 3:8).

Leer mense wat god
se hy is lief vir almal

en hy soek ons lewens.

> *Teach people what God says; He says He loves*
> *everyone, but He wants our lives.*

When God asks for our lives, He is asking our potsherds, for His mosaic.

The first message John the Baptist preached to prepare the way for Jesus was: *'Repent, for the kingdom of heaven is at hand!'* (Matthew 3:2). To me, this message means that holiness is necessary to enter the Kingdom of heaven. Repentance is when we lay down our lives, turn our back on sin, and walk into a new direction. Genuine repentance will bring about such a dramatic change in our lives, that if we look back, we won't be able to recognize the old man we left behind.

Rebirth is the starting point on the road of holiness, but then we need to bear the sweet fruit of repentance. That means: laying down our lives, dying to self, growing in Christ – in every area of our lives. Through this process, God will purify our hearts until we shine brightly! The road is definitely narrow, so don't expect anything else. To die to self is not easy, but everyone has to go through the purifying process.

Rebirth is when we make a choice to live sold-out to the King: to seek first the Kingdom of God and His righteousness (see Matthew 6:33). The *road of holiness* is when we keep on making this choice day after day.

All I can say is that God is good! His nature is one of mercy and great kindness. When we repent and change our ways, we will always find grace! He not only forgives, but He leaves a blessing. We don't always feel worthy of a blessing, but His Father-heart rejoices when one of His children returns to Him. Just like with the prodigal son, He will prepare a feast even if the son doesn't deserve it.

> 'Or do you despise the riches of His goodness,
> forbearance, and longsuffering,
> not knowing that the goodness of God
> leads you to repentance?'
> *- Romans 2:4 -*

This is the nature of God's love towards us. He knows that sin destroys our lives, and that is why He hates it so much. He doesn't force us to lay our lives down. Rather, He invites us through His goodness to repent and enter into His kingdom.

> 'Today, if you will hear His voice,
> do not harden your hearts as in the rebellion.'
> *- Hebrews 3:15 -*

When we hear the gentle voice of the Holy Spirit convicting us of sin, we must not harden our hearts. When He convicts us, we must repent and turn away as quickly as we can. Immediate obedience is a key step to experiencing His love, and hearing His voice every day. When we are obedient with little, then He will trust us with much. If we hear and obey His soft voice that says: *'Lay down. Turn around. Come back to Me,'* we will also hear and obey when He says: *'Receive. Hand out. Be My hands and feet. Experience the miracles, healings, and deliverances!'*

weet jy mamma wat hom gelukkig maak is gehoorsaamheid aan God

> *Do you know what pleases Jesus, Mommy?*
> *...Obedience to God.*

I am convinced that the level of our obedience to Jesus is determined by the level of our love for Him. Our love and our obedience will increase the more we surrender to Him. As His children, He wants to walk with us through life. He is a God of abundance. He always has more than enough for our needs, and a life of abundance is what He has in store for you and me.

Jesus is standing next to you right now, waiting to take your hand and lead you to His cross and into the Kingdom of heaven. Please, don't wait for a stop sign before you make your decision.

Father, forgive me as I forgive others

Wees Heilig vir Jesus
Wys asb mense dat hulle
moet God eer en
hom vrees asb mamma.
Hy is Heilig en hy
wys my wat vir hom
Walg is trots.
Weet mamma mammo
moet God asb eer
Hy wil jou lewe hê..
Lê jou voorop gestelde idees
neer, sal jy my glo. God is
Heilig, wees asb. asb. Heilig.

Be holy for Jesus.
Please show people they must honor God and fear Him.
Please, Mommy. God is holy, and He shows me
*what disgusts Him is **pride**.*
Mommy, you must please honor God.
He wants your life. Lay down your preconceived ideas.
Please believe me; God is holy. Please, please, be holy.

God has made it so easy for us to receive forgiveness. Everything we need is in the blood of the Lamb. Jesus paid the full price for the forgiveness of our sin and our salvation. We just need to receive it by faith.

But what about forgiving others?

For some reason, this is one of the most difficult things for people to do. When we pray: *'Forgive us our debts, as we forgive our debtors'* (Matthew 6:12), do we really realize what we are saying?

I once prayed for a woman and I couldn't help but notice that she had extremely bad breath. As I drove home that night, I asked the Lord what was wrong with her. Holy Spirit said, 'That is unforgiveness you smelled, Retha. It makes people rotten from the inside.' Streams of bitterness flowed from her inside, and I could smell it in her breath. Many sicknesses are rooted in unforgiveness; it is like drinking poison and then hoping someone else will get sick.

> *Please teach people that God wants their lives.*
> *Please show them what God shows you.*
> *Do you want to know what Jesus showed me?*
> *We always need to be obedient to Him.*
> *Please be obedient to Him.*
>
> *You will teach people forgiveness is necessary*
> *to enter the Kingdom of God.*
> *Please show people that we need*
> *to leave everything and follow Jesus.*
> *Know that God will never leave us nor forsake us, Mommy.*
> *You will go and tell the people that*
> *Jesus wants them to be ready.*

I have ministered to various people who are in situations similar to Aldo's: they are seriously incapacitated due to severe brain injuries. The spirit within them is still alive and well, but their souls (comprised of mind, will and emotions), and their flesh seem broken to the outside world. There are times when I visit special patients like this, and I feel the Holy Spirit's prompting to lift up their hands and help them write; just as I did in those early days with Aldo. With my own hand I will support and steady their palms while they form the letters. Through these letters, the people captured inside have a way to express themselves even if they can't speak. It is their spirit speaking through these letters. The things they write about, whether about their families or themselves, are so deep and true. Beautiful reconciliations have come out of these writings.

I once helped a man who had been struggling for years with the unforgiveness in his heart. Through his letter he said that he forgave the person who wronged him and asked the person's forgiveness in return. He also wrote: 'Jesus says if there is any unforgiveness in your heart, you can't enter heaven.'

There was no way that I could have known about all these personal details. (I only met him the day before in the hospital.) Until that day, this man could not speak, but now he communicates through his writings. I was so excited after his letter, because it showed me that even though he just sits in his wheelchair day after day, Jesus is still working with him and speaking to his spirit. From the outside, it might look as if he is no longer part of society, but believe me – he is alive! He is limited by his broken body, but his spirit speaks through his letters. If I had not helped him with his letter, he might never have been able to ask for forgiveness.

I know God has anointed me for this special type of work. It is the working of the Holy Spirit, and I can't explain it. I have walked the difficult road with my son, and I know firsthand what the person captured inside the broken body is going through. I see how people fight to believe these supernatural letters. To let go and give up hope is sometimes just so much easier. With modern technology there are new computers that put a voice to the words the patient types on the keyboard, and this is believable.

Why does God choose to speak through Aldo's letters? I don't have the answer. I do not even try to explain it anymore, because man will never be able to tell God what He can or cannot do. I know, that I know, that I know these writings are from God. In my heart I feel so sorry for people that point with a judgmental finger. They are judging the works of God! God is the God of the impossible, and nothing is too difficult for Him.

When I think back to Aldo's first letters that only captured his most basic needs — *hungry*, *thirsty*, and *Jesus will make me talk*, my heart breaks all over again. If I did not pick up his hand in faith during those days, I would never have known that people in his condition could write. I was desperate to find a way to communicate with him, and God made a way through the letters. It doesn't matter that he has a serious head injury; his spirit is still healthy.

Spirit is like a monetary currency. It doesn't matter if the money note (the body) is crumpled; the value stays the same. In the end, only our spirit has true value; our body stays behind. I am more interested in the condition of someone's spirit, than in the condition of his flesh. I would rather hear what his spirit has to say, than what his broken flesh has to say. This I see so clearly in Aldo – what he wants to say doesn't always come out the way he intends it to, but when he writes it comes from his spirit, straight from God's heart.

As can be expected, not everyone feels the same way. Friends would tell me about the stories they hear on the outside of people criticizing and throwing stones at these supernatural letters. Whenever I hear such I a report I am deeply hurt and I wonder to myself what it will take for people to start believing that God is the God of miracles. I cannot box and gift-wrap faith, to give it to anybody. It is each person's own responsibility to open their hearts and minds to the God of the impossible, because without faith it is impossible to please God (see Hebrews 11:6). You either believe or you don't, but there are consequences to what you decide. God can do anything, and He will do it – regardless of whether we understand it or not.

Naturally, I never tell Aldo when one of these stones hits, because I know it will hurt him – but he always picks it up in the Spirit:

You were hurt because of what he said.
Did you know he also said Jesus wasn't in your son?

> *God says you have to forgive him.*
> *He will protect you from such people.*
> *People and their works will be judged.*
> *God showed me He knows what people say,*
> *but He loves them. Did I do something wrong?*

This letter will always stay with me — God loves everyone! It doesn't matter if they hurt us; God still wants to save them and change them. The responsibility lies with those of us who have come to know the love and forgiveness of Jesus, to extend it to others; to forgive our enemies unconditionally and to bless them. The reason they are hurting us, might be because of their own hurt inside. We must have compassion and mercy and look at them through Jesus' eyes.

> 'But I say to you, love your enemies,
> bless those who curse you,
> do good to those who hate you, and pray
> for those who spitefully use you and persecute you.'
> *- Matthew 5:44 -*

> *I will forgive again, because that is*
> *what Jesus wants me to do.*
> *Mommy, you also need to forgive.*
> *Be what Jesus wants you to be — always be the least.*
> *God wants to teach us. Please listen to God, Mommy.*
> *Will you be like Samuel and do God's will, Mommy?*

Unforgiveness has its root in pride. Probably the biggest threat in our spiritual walk is pride. The Bible warns us: *'Pride goes before destruction, and a haughty spirit before a fall'* (Proverbs 16:18). Pride easily finds its way into our hearts, and is the most stubborn weed to get rid of. Pride is one of the main reasons we struggle to forgive others, because we feel entitled to stay hurt and angry. Self-justification withholds so many people from their victory. We must stop being stubborn and self-willed, seeking our own good all the time.

Wat sal jou so verder af
en verder van God af vat
Sonde soos trots.

> *What will take you further and further away from God?*
> *...Sin like pride.*

When I minister in very poor areas such as Africa, Asia, or Indonesia, I come face to face with people who are seeking God with pure motives. They don't seek Him for a better car or a bigger house, because there aren't any. They seek Him because He is the only Living God, and their only desire is to be one with Him. They walk for miles to attend the meetings, and will arrive hours early and only leave hours after the preaching has ended, just to spend more time in worship.

With humble spirits they call on the name of Jesus, and God has no alternative but to respond to the panting of their hearts. Believe me, they will keep on seeking until they find, keep on asking until He gives, and keep on knocking until Jesus Himself opens the door; because all they want is Him.

At one of these meetings, the magnificent glory of God descended as a cloud on us. This was the reward for their humility and their persistent seeking. From this cloud, signs, miracles, and wonders poured down as rain. Cancers were healed, the lame walked, and many testified of having open-heaven experiences.

In the Western world, luxury, tradition, and pride often suppress the flow of the Holy Spirit. I have ministered in many places saturated with worldly content and comfort where the anointing of the Holy Spirit could not flow in the same way as in these poor countries. People are hesitant to sing too loud or to respond to the altar call when I offer to pray for them. Everyone is looking around at what his or her neighbor is doing instead of looking only at Jesus.

The carnal man will try to 'stone' everything it can't explain. We need to make peace with the fact that the Creator of the universe is almighty, and He can do anything He wants. We will never be able to explain God's miracles or His ways that are so high above our own. God is Spirit, and to understand Him we need to look with our spirit and not with our flesh.

Self-righteousness is a fruit of pride. Through tradition, agendas, and dogma we can so easily place our religion in a man-made box that we forget about the Holy Spirit. It is then that *self* takes over. *Self* wants to declare its independence from God. *Self* wants to prove it is better than others. *Self* wants to make decisions according to human wisdom, regardless of what God says. *Self* walks over others to get into a better position. Self doesn't know how to love. *Self* only cares about *me, me, me*.

Wys hulle jy is Lief vir Jesus spreek hulle vry.

> *Show them that you love Jesus — forgive them.*

We must root out pride and self-righteousness in our lives and bind ourselves to the love of Jesus. The fragrance of our hearts is what makes us children of God, because it is out of the abundance of the heart that the mouth speaks. There are some who pretend to be what they are not, but when the fire of the trials of life come too close, true motives will be revealed. The storms of life have a way of revealing what is hidden. The heart of the King is one of love, compassion, mercy, and humility, and our aim must be for our hearts to be a mirror image of His.

'Love suffers long and is kind; love does not envy;
love does not parade itself, is not puffed up;
does not behave rudely, does not seek its own,
is not provoked, thinks no evil; does not rejoice in iniquity,
but rejoices in the truth; bears all things,
believes all things, hopes all things, endures all things.

> Love never fails....'
> - *1 Corinthians 13:4-8* -

You need to forgive in order to receive forgiveness. Forgiveness is a choice. You will not wake up one morning and suddenly feel like forgiving. You need to decisively go on your knees and forgive those people who wronged you.

Thank You, Jesus, that You showed us perfect love and perfect forgiveness when you hung on the cross and said, 'Forgive them, Father, they know not what they do' (see Luke 23:34). You are the perfect example, and showed us that love is perfected through forgiveness.

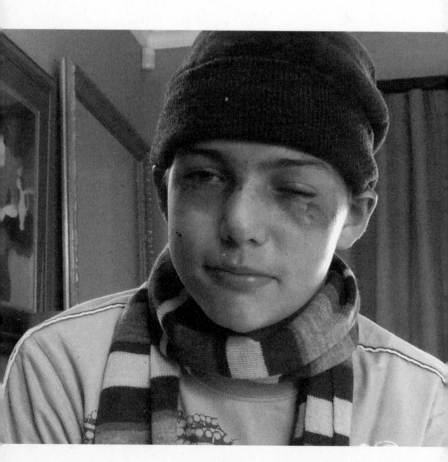

Overflowing with His Spirit

het jy na my verlang
want ek het. Wil jy weet
hoe seer ek gehad het.
ek voel baie beter.
my god se jy dink
jy was werklik so r
verkeerd maor jy is
hie wat god gese het
hy gaan doen sal hy
wysheid sal jy en ek
kry met god se werk
weet wat jy en ek
werk klaar vir God
hy se weet wat my
Lewe is hou met
met god weet het
wet het doodgemaak
maar gees lewe. god
het jou god se gees
wysheid gegee. werk asb

Did you miss me, Mommy? Because I missed you.
You have no idea how much pain I went through,
but I feel much better now. God says you think you were
wrong, but you are not. What God said He was going to do,
He will complete. We will receive wisdom to do God's work.
Do you know that you and I already work for God?
He says I should know that my life is now with Him.
You must know that the Law kills but the Spirit brings life.
God gave you His Spirit – Wisdom. Please work.

'God is Spirit, and those who worship Him,
must worship in spirit and truth.'
- John 4:24 -

To worship God in spirit and truth, you need to worship from a place I call 'in the Spirit' through your spirit. In contrast to this act of true worship, you can worship only through your flesh. When you worship 'in the Spirit' you will experience how you start living 'in the Spirit' (the Kingdom of Light) more and more. As you pray and worship in this new reality, you will become more aware of God's presence than of your outward circumstance.

See it as two rooms – the spirit room and the flesh room. You can stand in the flesh room and try to talk with God. This is very tiresome and there are many who try to do it this way. There you cry out as loud as you can, but it feels as if your prayers only reach the ceiling. People then complain that they can't hear God's voice or that their prayers aren't heard.

Through the blood of Jesus, God has made a way for each of us to enter into the 'spirit-room' and worship Him in spirit and truth. As you enter this room blood-washed, you have access to kneel in front of the throne of grace. There you will definitely hear His voice! The choice to walk through this door is in each person's own hands. No one can make that choice for you, but the opportunity is there for all of us.

Hebrews 4:14-16 describes this 'spirit-room' beautifully: *'Seeing then that we have a great High Priest who has passed through the heavens, Jesus the Son of God, let us hold fast our confession. For we do not have a High Priest who cannot sympathize with our weaknesses, but was in all points tempted as we are, yet without sin. Let us therefore come boldly to the throne of grace, that we may obtain mercy and find grace to help in time of need.'*

This 'spirit-room' is especially built for worship. It doesn't necessarily mean that you worship 'in the Spirit' only when you sing in your Spirit-language (the Holy-Spirit-inspired tongue). I believe true worship is when you worship God in such a manner that your entire being is focused on Him and your heart pants to bring Him glory – to see Him smile over you, while you are lifting His name high.

The moment worship becomes a ritual, and we get into a rut of singing two fast songs, followed by two slow songs, and then turning to our brother or sister to shake their hand; we have lost true worship and engage only in a habit. When we truly worship God from the spirit-room, we will find our way right into the throne room. There we will receive the revelation knowledge and the answers to our prayers that we so desperately seek.

There, in the spirit-room, the miracles take place. There you are filled with God's Spirit and your own spirit gets renewed. It is the place where you receive His joy, peace, wisdom, healing for a broken heart and body, and there you will hear His voice crystal clear. It is also a place of fellowship, where you can talk to God and share your heart. Here your spiritual eyes are open and you talk to God, spirit to Spirit. To me it is a place of few words, lots of tears, joy, peace, and healing. It is a place of repentance and intimacy, where the King shares His heart with His Bride.

Once you have entered this spirit-room you will never want to leave. And you don't have to! God made it possible for you to live in the Spirit, not only visiting Him there once in a while. This asks commitment. To walk in the Spirit '24/7' requires that you take your eyes off worldly things and focus only on God's heart, His character, and His will for your life. Faith in God will come automatically if you do this, because His character will become a reality in your life. In the spirit-room you will pray as if you were sitting on Your Father's lap. He is no longer far away, but you are sitting with Him in heavenly places.

Look closely what Hebrews 4:16 says: *'Let us therefore **come boldly** to the throne of grace, that we may obtain mercy and find grace to help in time of need.'* The responsibility to draw close to God is in our hands. The cross of Jesus made the way for us to go boldly to the throne of grace ourselves. Why do we still want someone else to go in for us? Why are we satisfied with someone else's description of His heartbeat? Jesus wants each and every one of us to come in, and become one with Him.

In the Spirit is where things are determined. There, in His throne room, and in His courts, is where your future is being formed. The foundation to walking in the Spirit, is a hunger and thirst to know God and to have a holy and pure heart. It all starts with a desire. The cross of Jesus is the way God made for us to a pure, blood-washed, life. The cross is the key to a life lived by walking according to the Spirit and not the lusts of the flesh, because the cross is the bridge between the flesh and the spirit.

In the spirit-room there are also spiritual anointings, blessings, weapons, and gifts. Anointings on your life come from the throne of grace and the Holy Spirit administers them from there. Whatever gift you receive from God in the Spirit, is given so that you can glorify the King through your gift. It is given so you can be the hands and feet of Jesus here on earth – to pray for the sick, to preach the Gospel, and even to do greater works than Jesus did (see John 14:12).

One day Aldo asked me: 'Mommy, do you still pray for me?'

'Of course Aldo, why do you ask?'

He answered, 'Because, in heaven God sends out His angels to help when people pray.'

In Acts 12 this powerful result of prayer is confirmed. Peter was arrested and put in prison, but all the while the church offered up constant prayer for him to God (see Acts 12:5).

In answer to their prayers, God sent an angel to open the gates of the prison and lead Peter out to safety.

Remember, the effective, fervent prayer of a righteous man avails much (see James 5:16). So much so, that prison gates will be opened and angels will appear. When you pray in the spirit-room, expect miracles!

The spirit-room is also where you get to know the Holy Spirit intimately. Acts 2:1-4 describes the first baptism of the Holy Spirit: *'And when the day of Pentecost had fully come, they were all assembled together in one place, when suddenly there came a sound from heaven like the rushing of a violent tempest blast, and it filled the whole house in which they were sitting. And there appeared to them tongues resembling fire, which were separated and distributed and which settled on each one of them. **And they were all filled (diffused throughout their souls) with the Holy Spirit and began to speak in other... languages (tongues), as the Spirit kept giving them clear and loud expression...'** (AMP).

This infilling of the Holy Spirit kept on flowing until each person overflowed with it. People came running from the streets to see what had happened. This tells me there is a difference between *knowing about* the Holy Spirit and *being filled* with Him.

In Acts 19, Paul makes the following statement about the infilling of the Holy Spirit: *"Did you receive the Holy Spirit when you believed?" So they said to him, "We have not so much as heard whether there is a Holy Spirit." And he said to them, "Into what then were you baptized?" So they said, "Into John's baptism." Then Paul said, "John indeed baptized with a baptism of repentance, saying to the people that they should believe on Him who would come after him, that is, on Christ Jesus." When they heard this, they were baptized in the name of the Lord Jesus. **And when Paul had laid hands on them, the Holy Spirit came upon them, and they spoke with tongues and prophesied'** (Acts 19:2-6).

The first martyr for Christ, Stephen, is a wonderful example of someone who overflowed with the Holy Spirit. The Holy Spirit dwelt inside of Him and opened his eyes to see beyond the natural. He was the only person who saw Jesus standing next to the Father, while the others were busy collecting stones to kill him. The Holy Spirit will not only open your eyes, but He will also change your heart. Stephen didn't condemn his murderers. His heart was changed to reflect Jesus' heart and that is why he said (as he knelt down to die): '"Lord, do not charge them with this sin." And when he had said this, he fell asleep' (Acts 7:60 b).

> God says what is happening now is I am very tired.
> Wisdom shows me I mustn't drink wine,
> because people shouldn't be drunk from wine
> but be filled with the Holy Spirit.
> Jesus showed me He gave us the Holy Spirit.
> Will you please help me,
> because I must be one with Him every day?
> God says you have entrusted my life to Him.

Ephesians 5:18 says: 'Do not be drunk with wine, in which is dissipation; but be filled with the Spirit...'

Once again, it comes down to choices – the cup of the world or the cup of Christ. When we drink from the cup of the world, we can expect our perspective to change to a worldly perspective. Have you noticed that a person's personality changes when they drink a bit too much? When this happens we become easy targets for the enemy, because our guard isn't up.

In the same manner, your character will change when you drink from the cup of the Holy Spirit. Just like Stephen, you will be able to forgive and love, no matter what happens. The fruit of the Spirit will automatically bloom in your life. As it becomes part of who you are, you will no longer have to glue Galatians 5:22-23 to your mirror to remind yourself every day to walk in love, joy, peace, patience, kindness, goodness, faithfulness, gentleness, and self-control.

Be wise, and turn your back on the world's ways of dealing with the storms of life — by trying to escape the pain, or by drowning it out with temporary pleasures. Also be aware that if you are drunk from the world's cup, you aren't as vigilant against temptations, compromises, and the attacks of the enemy. The cup of Christ holds the wine of the Holy Spirit and eternal life.

Abba Father is my Daddy, and I run to Him for protection and provision. Jesus is my Beloved and through His perfect love, I have learned what true love is, but I only came to know and understand Holy Spirit much later, even though He has always been with me. In order to walk in the fullness of God, it is important for us to know each person of the God-head intimately.

I was scheduled for another speaking engagement in Asia, my second trip to the East in one year. The afternoon before I went on stage, I sought the Lord's face to hear what message He had on His heart for His people. There on the floor of my hotel room, God had a divine encounter in store for me that I definitely didn't expect: I was to meet the Holy Spirit in a surprising new way.

I heard the Father say to my spirit, 'Retha, I don't want you to do anything, go anywhere, or say one word without My Holy Spirit. Don't let human tradition, your watch, or schedules determine your steps – wait on His guidance. Invite Him to go before you and prepare the way. You must be obedient to My voice and not make compromises to follow man-made ideas. My Holy Spirit dwells in you and His power will flow though you as you walk in obedience. My Holy Spirit will reveal the secrets of My heart to you.'

As I lay face down on the floor, seeking the Holy Spirit with new zeal, a whirlwind came into the room, and I was shaken with these words: 'Retha, I am not "*the* Holy Spirit." You can call me "Holy Spirit." I am personal. I am not far off. I am in you. I want to be your best Friend, your Counselor, your Advocate, and your Comforter. You are filled with My power, and when you move in obedience to My voice, I can move mountains through you. Know this – you are never, ever alone. I am always with you. You and I are one.'

The wind kept blowing, and I cried uncontrollably in

the awe of this amazing experience. After some time, I got up and started preparing for the service that was about to start. On my way to the service, I talked to my best Friend with the intimacy I only discovered moments before. He had always been there in the past, but I never had such an awareness of His awesome presence the way I did now.

'Retha, all you need to do is invite Me in. Only I can change the hearts of the people. At the precise moment you need direction, you will hear a voice behind you saying turn to the right or turn to the left. Don't be afraid, trust Me. I will be with you wherever you go. I will lead you and guide you. Through your obedience, you will be led into the abundant life that the Father has planned for you.'

While I stood on the stage I heard the Holy Spirit say: 'Retha, I want you to anoint all these people tonight.'

I wondered if I heard Him correctly. Did Holy Spirit see how many people were standing before me? I skeptically looked down into my bag at the small bottle of anointing oil that I usually carry with me.

I thought to myself, 'The Lord is going to have to do a miracle tonight if every person is to receive some of this oil!'

Holy Spirit gently reassured me: 'Retha, look at your hands. I don't need your oil that comes in a man-made bottle. I dwell inside of you, and I am the anointing.' As I looked down, I saw His anointing oil already covering my hands. I could only weep in astonishment. 'Lord, You are truly alive! How will I ever begin to understand Your greatness?'

I walked down the steps to anoint the first group of people.

'Just put your hands out toward them, Retha,' I heard the voice of Holy Spirit directing me again.

As I obeyed His instruction, they fell to the ground as the power of God took over. Speechless, I stood looking at what just happened. Holy Spirit spoke to me again, 'I will go before you and prepare the way. All I am looking for is an obedient heart that loves Me. You must believe that the Lion of Judah lives inside of you.'

This experience in Asia made me hungry for more.

From that moment on, I have pursued this tangible intimacy with Holy Spirit every day. Our love relationship has become so real to me. Best of all, I only have to ask if I don't know. Holy Spirit always answers! To walk in the Spirit means Holy Spirit directs your every step.

Waar sal God mense kry wat
Hom in gees en in waarheid
aanbid. Sal ons God se goods
kinders wees. Word soos God
beplan het vir ons lewe.

> Where will God find people willing to worship Him
> in spirit and truth? Will we be God's children?
> We need to become what God has planned for our lives.
> We will become like God – holy.

One day we were walking through the streets of New York, Holy Spirit and I, and He whispered in my ear, 'Always remember, love is not action, but passion. Jesus wants His Bride to love Him with a pure and holy passion! There is only one love language that makes the heart of the Bridegroom rejoice – obedience. You will walk in obedience when you serve and love your brothers without expecting anything in return. Retha, just be yourself when you are with Me. I enjoy being with you and flowing through you. I will flow though those who trust Jesus and are totally sold out to Him. I am the flame that makes your heart burn with passion for the King of kings.'

Holy Spirit is the fire of God inside of Me. He never sleeps, and He causes my spirit to be awake even while my body is asleep. I go to bed praying in my heavenly language, knowing that Holy Spirit will speak with my spirit throughout the night. When I dream, He makes me lie down in fields of lilies (my favorite flowers), and He shows me what I look like through God's eyes.

Holy Spirit is truly my best Friend. He shows me secret places in the Spirit and He teaches me about what happens before the throne. He comforts me when I cry and holds me when I get hurt. But more than that, He laughs with me and helps me to enjoy life. In every situation, for every question, Holy Spirit holds the key to the answer, because He is our wisdom from God. Once we are filled and overflowing with Holy Spirit, Romans 8:16 is transformed from Logos (the written Word) to Rhema (the living Word) in our hearts: *'The Spirit Himself bears witness with our spirit that we are children of God.'*

> *God says those who love God will also love their neighbor.*
> *What is your hurt? Because Jesus wants to heal it.*
> *He wants to use us to bring His fire.*

I once again had to go and minister and Holy Spirit whispered into my ear, 'Retha, take a closer look at the crowd sitting in front of you. You will see where I move among the people. As I touch their hearts, you will be able to see the change.'

Sure enough, the moment I knew what to look for I could see where Holy Spirit was touching and changing hearts. It came like a wave, and I could recognize the reactions as He touched their hearts in different ways. With my spiritual eyes I could see the flames falling from heaven and I knew some people were experiencing His holy fire. Some were shaking, others were crying, and some fell down under His power. There were also those who only felt His presence through His peace that rested on them, without an outward manifestation.

The touch of the Spirit is an undeniable force – there is nothing like it. Sometimes people ask me why they didn't experience the presence of the Holy Spirit in the same way someone else did by shaking or falling down. I always tell them each person is unique and the Holy Spirit works with each one of us differently. Even if nothing happened immediately – God still worked! All honor belongs to the Lord, because no person can fully comprehend or take credit for the work He does in the hearts of men.

One night, while I was praying in my hotel room before yet another event, Holy Spirit prepared me for what was to come. 'Retha, expect to see a river flowing through the church tonight. When you see it, stop preaching and give over to Me.'

After ministering only a few minutes, I could see with my spiritual eyes, the river flowing from God's throne through the church. Revelation 22, which I read the previous evening, suddenly became alive in my heart. I made the invitation: 'Anyone who is looking for more of God – come to the front. Holy Spirit is showing me the river is here, and for all those who seek it, come to the front and jump in!'

For two hours the Holy Spirit flowed freely, touching people in different ways. The river of God brought new life to dry and weary souls!

As with any relationship, as you grow in love and become more intimate, you learn what makes your Beloved happy and also what causes Him pain. Later, when the two of you are so close, you will hurt when He is hurt, because the two of you have become one. When people criticize the works of Holy Spirit, I feel the pain in my own heart and it makes me want to cry. When you walk in the Spirit with Him, the workings of Holy Spirit will no longer be strange to you, but as natural as daylight. It is when people walk in the flesh and their eyes are only accustomed to darkness, that the light of God's glory hurts their eyes and they criticize what they don't understand. Fearful, people then cry: 'Switch off the lights!' But it is the light that drives out the darkness.

Yes, Holy Spirit can definitely be grieved.

'And do not grieve the Holy Spirit of God, by whom you were sealed for the day of redemption. Let all bitterness, wrath, anger, clamor, and evil speaking be put away from you, with all malice. And be kind to one another, tenderhearted, forgiving one another, even as God in Christ forgave you.'
- *Ephesians 4:30-32* -

I walk in relationship with Holy Spirit and I can't tell Him enough how much I love Him. I don't need to force myself to do this, it comes naturally...it *overflows*.

Holy Spirit, I long for Your touch. Please cover me, fill me and heal my broken heart…
Holy Spirit, You are the Spirit of truth. Please read this book with me and tell me what You think…
Holy Spirit, what does this passage of Scripture really mean?…
Holy Spirit, what do You think of this situation, and what must I do?…
Holy Spirit, tell me more about My Bridegroom… I love Him so much, and You know all there is to know about Him…
Holy Spirit, we are going to Namibia!…
Holy Spirit, we are going to count the stars tonight. Please will You join us and teach me more about the greatness of my Almighty God?…
Holy Spirit, You are most precious…
You are my everything. Without You, I am only dust.

And so I talk to Holy Spirit about everything in my life – big and small.

People ask me how long I pray before I know the power of God will manifest. That is not how it works for me. God lives in me. When I pray, He is there. When I don't pray, He is there. All I have to do is to stay in the Spirit, walk in obedience, and the power will flow.

While doing some shopping one afternoon, a lady walked up to me in the mall and asked me to pray for her. 'Sorry, Ma'am, but I don't think now is the best time', I answered 'I know when I lift my hand God's power is going to flow and there is a good chance you might end up on the floor.'

The only reason I gave such a bold answer is because I know the Lion of Judah is living inside of me. It wasn't that I didn't want to pray for her, I just wanted her to understand what could happen when the power of God flows. That is what it means to live in the Spirit – to know that the Kingdom of God is not words, but power. Only 'in the Spirit' will we receive the victory we are seeking after. That is why Paul says: *'Walk in the Spirit, and you shall not fulfill the lust of the flesh'* (Galatians 5:16).

> 'The grace of the Lord Jesus Christ, and the love of God
> and the *communion* of the Holy Spirit be with you all…'
> *- 2 Corinthians 13:14 -*

Communion is fellowship with Holy Spirit. How I just love being in His presence! Sometimes, I run to the prayer room in my office (or any room I can find) just to fall on my face before Him, and say: 'Father, Son, and Holy Spirit, with all my being I adore You!' The more time I spend with Him, and the more I know about Him, the more I fall in love with Him.

Holy Spirit and I travel the world together ministering. We talk on the airplane, and He tells me what to expect and helps me to pray effectively. His wisdom is my compass. The sevenfold Holy Spirit before the throne of God teaches me everything I need to know (see Revelation 1:4). The seven Spirits are described in Isaiah 11 verse 2: *'The **Spirit of the LORD** shall rest upon Him, the Spirit of **wisdom** and **understanding**, the Spirit of **counsel** and **might**, the Spirit of the **knowledge** and of the **fear of the LORD.**'*

The more I experience the joy of knowing He is pleased with me, the more I want to please Him! In Him I have my peace. I can't go before the throne, into the presence of God, without Holy Spirit. I can't even say, 'Jesus, I love you!' without Holy Spirit. We need to understand that without Him we are totally empty. When we cherish and prize His presence above all other earthly relationships, we will move into the fullness of our relationship with Father God and Jesus.

> 'There is therefore now no condemnation
> to those who are in Christ Jesus, who do not walk according to
> the flesh, but according to the Spirit.
> For the law of the Spirit of life in Christ Jesus
> has made me free from the law of sin and death'
> *- Romans 8:1-2 -*

The Spirit seals our adoption into the family of God as sons of the Most High, and through the Spirit of adoption we can boldly call the King of the universe our Abba Father. The Word also says that as many as are led by God, these are the sons of God. (See Romans 8:14-15.) That is what I call myself – son of God!

The enemy will try to steal the privileges of 'sonship', because in 'sonship' there is freedom and liberty. A son will boldly run to the arms of His Daddy when he is hurt or scared. Satan tries to steal this freedom by continually reminding the sons of God of their unworthiness and that they don't deserve this adoption. What Satan is trying to do, is to get us to feel like slaves, not sons. When this happens, we should run to the throne of grace and call out to our Abba Father who has already accepted us as His sons (see Hebrews 4:16).

The law of the Spirit is liberty! As sons in the house of our Father, we have the liberty to learn and mature without having to fear that our Father will stop loving us. When we make mistakes, He will definitely discipline us (for our own good), but He will never stop loving us (see Hebrews 12:5-10).

I minister in so many churches that are still in slavery to tradition, rules, and man-made laws. A lot of people reject the workings of the Holy Spirit, because they have never experienced them before. Even today, people still pick up stones to throw at things they don't understand, can't explain, or haven't experienced themselves — just as in Stephen's story in Acts 7. I have heard stories of leaders making excuses for when Holy Spirit moved in a traditional church. With tears in my eyes I cry out, 'Lord help me! Where I go, You go with me – because we are one. I can't limit what You want to do, and I don't want to!'

The Lord's answer is always the same: 'Retha, pray for them and bless them.'

I know this power and anointing doesn't come from myself, it can only come from God and all I can do is stand back and hand over to Him.

> 'Not that we are sufficient of ourselves
> to think of anything as being from ourselves,
> but our sufficiency is from God,
> who also made us sufficient as ministers of the new covenant,
> not of the letter but of the Spirit, for the letter kills,
> but the Spirit gives life.'
> - *2 Corinthians 3:5-6* -

> *You were where Jesus was when He was rejected by men.*
> *He shows me who hurt you.*
> *Jesus wants to show you what legalism does to people.*
> *Teach them like Moses taught the people about God's power,*
> *so that everyone there will now seek God's power.*
> *You must preach again like you did last night.*
> *Jesus says you will stand up,*
> *and what He asks of you, you will do.*

At the same time, I also want to warn the sons of God never to misuse this liberty, freedom, and grace we have as children in our Father's house. Never use grace and liberty as an excuse for sin. The grace of God is not there so we can justify sin, but rather to keep us from sinning. Grace is our victory over sin, not the rug we sweep it under. Paul says in Romans 6:14-16: *'For sin shall not have dominion over you, for you are not under law but under grace. What then? Shall we sin because we are not under law but under grace? Certainly not! Do you not know that to whom you present yourselves slaves to obey, you are that one's slaves whom you obey, whether of sin leading to death, or of obedience leading to righteousness?'*

At the end of the day it all comes down to love. In John 14:15 Jesus says: *'If you love Me, keep My commandments.'* Jesus directly links love with obedience. When you love Him, your desire will be to please Him, and your desire to please Him (through obedience) is your victory over sin. Find His grace and love at the foot of the cross and there you will also find your victory over sin.

> 'For if you live according to the flesh you will die; but if by the Spirit you put to death the deeds of the body, you will live.'
> *- Romans 8:13 -*

Holy Spirit is the fire of God. Holy fire. Heavenly fire. All-consuming fire. This fire will engrave the Word of God and His commandments on your heart, so you can live according to His will. The fire of God is a precious gift from the Father, but this fire is meant to be put on a lamp stand so it can give light to the world around you. This light will lead others to the source of light – Jesus. The brighter the fire burns, the more oil you will receive to keep the fire blazing, and the stronger the anointing will be on your life.

'John answered, saying to all,
"I indeed baptize with water,
but One mightier than I is coming,
whose sandal strap I am not worthy to loose.
He will baptize you with the *Holy Spirit* and *fire*."'
- *Luke 3:16* -

This baptism of the Holy Spirit and fire was not only for Biblical times – Jesus wants to give it to His Bride even today! But only dead wood can burn. That is why we need to put to death the deeds of the flesh so Jesus' resurrection power can flow through us.

God het Sy gees vir ons gegee om ons te ons te help met alles wat ons mee sukkel. Ons sal gaan en dan sal ons ons self aan God offer. Ek is lief vir jou mamma. God het my terug gestuur om vir die wereld te vertel dat Jesus leef. Ons moet gehoorsaam wees en lewe spreek. Sal mamma asb. altyd gehoorsaam wees en doen wat Jesus sal wys.

Jesus gives us a significant promise that the Holy Spirit will be given to anyone who asks:

'If a son asks for bread from any father among you,
will he give him a stone?
Or if he asks for a fish,
will he give him a serpent instead of a fish?
Or if he asks for an egg, will he offer him a scorpion?

If you then, being evil,
know how to give good gifts to your children,
how much more will your heavenly Father
give the Holy Spirit to those who ask Him!'
- Luke 11:11-13 -

From all the things you can receive from the Father, the Holy Spirit is the gift above all gifts. When the fire of the Holy Spirit burns in your heart, you have a treasure of much more worth than any earthly riches.

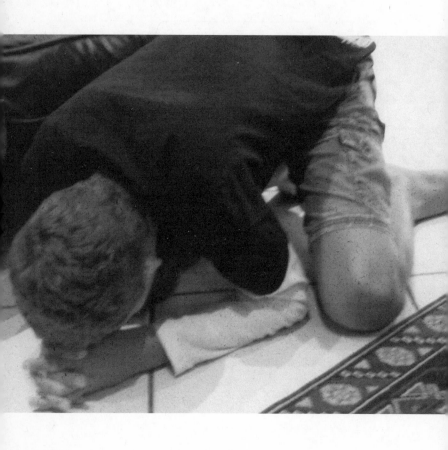

His name is Wisdom

Weet jy ander wil
wees en wer hê wat
ek het. Dit is daar vir
almal . My wysheid kom
van God af. Luister
na die Heilige Gees
Leer mense wat wysheid
is weet jy wat wil
God my geleer het
Hy sê ek is Sy
profeet en ek moet
my lewe gan hom gee
Jesus se wysheid is
van god my

Do you know other people want to be like me and want
what I have? It is there for everyone.
My wisdom comes from God.
Listen to the Holy Spirit.
Teach people what Wisdom is.
God wants to teach me and He says I am His prophet.
I must give my life to Him.
Jesus says wisdom is from God.

'Retha,' my best Friend, Holy Spirit, speaks to me again, 'all the spiritual gifts are inside of you. My Word in you will manifest with power on the outside. Everything you need to overcome is already inside of you, because My Kingdom is inside of you. Always remember, the greatest gift of all is My love – because love overcomes all.'

So many times people have told me they desire the gifts of the Spirit. There are nine gifts of the Spirit and nine fruit of the Spirit. Be obedient with the fruit of the Spirit (see Galatians 5:22-23), and God will entrust you with the gifts of the Spirit (see 1 Corinthians 12:4-11). A tree is known by its fruit, and thereafter the Holy Spirit gives the gifts as it pleases Him.

Jesus wil wys heid gee mense weet nie wie Hy is nie. hulle ken ook nie sy krag nie.

> *Jesus wants to give Wisdom,*
> *but people don't know who He is.*
> *Also, they don't know His power.*

'that the God of our Lord Jesus Christ,
the Father of glory, may give to you the spirit of wisdom and
revelation in the knowledge of Him,
the eyes of your understanding being enlightened;
that you may know what is the hope of His calling,
what are the riches of the glory of His inheritance in the saints,
and what is the exceeding greatness of His power
toward us who believe…'
- *Ephesians 1:17-19* -

Late one night while Aldo was already fast asleep, I went to tuck him in before going to bed myself. To my surprise, I saw his face covered with a golden glow. As I stared at my son, God revealed something new to me about His glory. If the Holy Spirit of God lives inside of us, we are vessels of the glory of God in us. It will reflect on our faces and emanate from our beings, because we are connected to Him. The more we are connected to Jesus, the more we will see His glory, and the more His glory will be reflected through us. If we keep on looking into the mirror of His Word, we will be changed from glory to glory into His image.

> *God will show you what He wants you to see.*
> *Jesus says I must worship and praise Him.*
> *He will give you wisdom again regarding His will.*
> *Do you have a job for me? I don't know what I am going to do after school. Did you see Him last night?*
> *Jesus says you will see in the Spirit.*

As the waiting years for Aldo's healing have been prolonged, his letters have evolved as he has matured through different seasons in his life. Lately, he has been referring to Holy Spirit as *Wisdom* in his letters. When he speaks of Holy Spirit, this is his favorite way to describe Him.

When the Lord asked Solomon what his heart's desire was, he answered: *'Give to Your servant an understanding heart to judge Your people, that I my discern between good and evil...'* (1 Kings 3:9). Solomon asked for wisdom and this pleased God. In fact, God was so pleased with his answer, that He gave him all the other blessings he could have asked for, as a reward. The lesson we need to learn from Solomon is that God smiles on His children when they seek wisdom from a pure heart.

We have also received the gift of Wisdom (that God gave to Solomon) – Holy Spirit, our wisdom from God! Jesus says of Holy Spirit: *'But the Helper, the Holy Spirit, whom the Father will send in My name, He will teach you all things, and bring to your remembrance all things that I said to you'* (John 14:26).

> *Show me what we must do for You.*
> *I will go and do what You ask me to do.*

> *God says we must trust Him with what*
> *He started in us because He will finish it.*
> *Do you know that Wisdom*
> *will guide you as you write the book?*
> *God will show what you must say to people.*
> *God will blow His Holy Spirit into the book.*
> *Please be obedient when God speaks.*

Sometimes, I sense *Wisdom* standing in the background, keeping an eye on me, to see how I will react in a certain situation. Whenever I sense His presence in this way, I know a test is coming. In order to pass the test, I need to ask for His perspective and His help.

'If any of you lacks wisdom, let him ask of God, who gives to all liberally and without reproach, and it will be given to him.

But let him ask in faith, with no doubting, for he who doubts is like a wave of the sea driven and tossed by the wind.'
- James 1:5-6 -

But, to be honest, I have learned a lot of lessons the hard way – by making mistakes.

'Oh, Holy Spirit, I failed again! Please help me,' I plead.

He always reassures me, 'Remember, I will never leave you nor forsake you. That is what I am here for – to help you when you stumble, and to lead you into truth. Whenever you stumble, repent and get back up again. Thank Me for the grace you know I have already given you. I will never deny grace and mercy to those who ask. Stay close to Me, My beloved. Keep your mantle of humility on. It is so important. Run from pride. Run! Pride is an enemy of the cross and will cause you to stumble. In Me, you have the liberty to be yourself, and I have the liberty to change you into a unique reflection of Christ. I made you one of a kind, so don't try to be like anybody else. Stay close to Me, and don't exchange My truth for the opinion of man.'

> *Be wise, He says. Receive wisdom from Wisdom.*
> *He shows me you are very tired from all your work.*
> *With Him you will find true rest. God shows me*
> *you want to please Him with all your heart.*
> *Ma'am, Wisdom says you have done your job well.*
> *Just be calm. I know how you feel now. God loves you.*

Pride is the archenemy of Wisdom. Pride says: I know better and I can make it on my own. I don't need any help.' But Wisdom says: *'...God resists the proud, but gives grace to the humble'* (1 Peter 5:5).

Wisdom will teach us all we need to know. What is more, He is also our Help so we can accomplish what He teaches us to do. Humility is the key to staying in fellowship with Wisdom.

> '...Therefore, I will all the more gladly glory in my weaknesses and infirmities, that the strength and power of Christ... may rest [yes, may pitch a tent over and dwell] upon me!'
> *- 2 Corinthians 12:9 (AMP) -*

I can honestly say that I am an excellent example of God's grace. If you had known the old Retha, you would agree with me, that there is no end to His grace. He freed me from so many things! To live *in* Him is to continually dwell in a tent of grace. There we will begin to understand that everything we receive (from the smallest blessing to the biggest breakthrough), is all by His grace – not because we deserve it. Every breath and each new day is grace from God!

Grace will lead us to humility, which will lead us to more grace. *Grace* is not our excuse for sin; rather, *grace* will teach us the value of obedience. *Grace* will never justify sin. *Grace* is given so that we can overcome sin.

If there is an area of sin in your life that you struggle with, do not treat it casually and try to sweep it under the rug (calling the rug the grace of God). Bring the sin to the light and ask God to strengthen you and help you to overcome. You will then receive *grace*, so you can be obedient to His will, and *mercy* and *forgiveness* for the mistakes of the past. Not even the worst imaginable sin-bondage is too difficult for Jesus to break – His grace is enough and His love overcomes all!

> *Do you know I saw Jesus?*
> *He said you asked Him for new strength.*
> *Jesus says you must know my future is in His hands.*
> *He says you want to please Him.*
> *Please wait for Wisdom from God.*
> *He will show you what to do.*
> *Do you know, Mommy, I will help you with the ministry?*
> *I was so relieved when you told me*
> *I will be working for your ministry. Thanks, Mommy.*

Wisdom will teach us: It is not about what we can get from others, but what we can give them. This is how God's Kingdom operates – to serve others. He will teach us how to serve; because servants are the true kings. He will teach us to walk by faith and not by sight, because what we see with our natural eyes is only temporary. He will teach us to fight with the one weapon that can never fail – Love. He will help us to embrace our cross, because only those who are willing to carry their cross can follow Jesus. Wisdom will only be a Rabbi (Teacher) to the humble – because they are the only ones willing to be taught.

Luister na god se stem. Dan sal jy sien hoe god werk wees asb gehoorsaam word God se hande en voete. hy wil sy krag vrystel

> *Listen to God's voice. Then you will see how He works.*
> *Please be obedient. Be God's hands and feet.*
> *He wants to let His power flow.*

Wisdom speaks to my heart and says: 'This bitter cup you are drinking from on your road with Aldo is a blessing. It keeps you humble, and that is why My power can flow through you. Don't resent the cup or wish it away. Remember, My grace is sufficient for you.'

Yes, Lord – Your grace is all I need. Please let me always dwell in Your tent of grace. Keep me from self-centeredness and pride; they only want to lure me to the outside. I just want to love You more and more, my King. I surrender my weakness to You, so Your strength can be made perfect in Me. Holy Spirit – Spirit of Truth – please lead me into Your truth.

WISDOM dwells in a tent of GRACE, which only the HUMBLE may enter. Wisdom, Humility and Grace are inseparable — find one, and you find the others.

Faith –
Believing is seeing

Jy sal weer my self en ek sal
gesond word God is baie lief
vir my en ook vir julle.
Weet mamma dat ons
word meer en meer soos
Jesus wys asb vir mense
my dagboek en wat
Jesus sê deur sy gees.
Weet mamma ons sal
Jesus wil gelukkig maak
as ons weet wat Hy
vir ons gedoen het aan
die kruis. Asb. mamma
sal jy glo dat ek sal
gesond word ek weet
God sal dit doen en My
alleen sal die eer kry
Hy vra of jy asb god sal
vertrou met ons toekoms?
Wees rustig mamma gaan sien ek
gaan gesond wees.

> *You will anoint me with oil again and I will be healed.*
> *God loves me very much;*
> *I also love you very much.*
> *Mommy, do you know that we are becoming more*
> *and more like Jesus?*
> *Please show all the people my journal*
> *and what Jesus says through His Spirit.*
> *Mommy, do you know that we will*
> *want to make Jesus happy if we understand*
> *what He did for us on the cross?*
> *Please, Mommy. Will you believe that I will be healed?*
> *I know God is going to do it, and He will receive all the honor.*
> *He asks if you will trust Him with our future?*
> *Relax, Mommy. You will see that I am going to be healed.*

…The just shall live by faith.
- Romans 1:17 -

What oxygen does for your flesh, so faith does for your spirit. Without even thinking about it, you continually breathe in and out every day. A few minutes without air and your entire body will shut down and die. In the same way, your spirit *breathes* faith.

When a person talks about faith, they only have to speak a few sentences for me to discern if they have head knowledge about the subject, or if their spirit breathes it daily. It is easy to talk about faith, but to live by faith is something else entirely.

To live by faith asks a price. When you take the first step out of the boat and onto the water, you cannot dare look at yourself, or rely on your own abilities. Your eyes need to be fixed on the One with whom nothing is impossible; the One who is standing on the water calling you towards Him.

Aldo was blind in the one eye for a long time after the accident, but the open eye had something I had never seen before. It glistened with hope. This hope is spelled: JESUS IS

ALIVE! Many people testify of the light they see when he looks at them with his one eye.

> *Where will my help come from, my help comes from the Lord the creator of the heavens and the earth. I will work and play as I always did. Show the people what Jesus shows you. I know that Jesus wants to shower you with a river of His power. My God will blow His Spirit over you, because you want to experience more of His power.*

Jesus and I have an intimate love relationship, and I can only walk this road of faith because of His love that carries me. Through His eyes, He lets me see beyond appearances, to discern the condition of the heart. Jesus wants to take our stony hearts, and give us new hearts filled with a new purpose (see Ezekiel 36:26-27). When our hearts are broken or hardened we must go to the only One who can heal or replace this precious possession. But no one can go for you – each person is responsible to take his or her own heart to the King.

When no one had any hope for Aldo, the 'impossibility' of the situation threatened to crush me. My faith in God built a protective wall around me, so that fear and hopelessness couldn't get to me. I still see how fear and hopelessness want to climb over this wall, even after all this time. But, Jesus fights for me. My faith is built on the Rock, and that is why the wall is unshakable.

There have been a lot of disappointments on our faith-road, usually because we took our eyes of Jesus and focused on someone or something else (even if it was just for a moment). It didn't matter that we exercised according to the best training program, or attended the best courses for brain injuries; at the end of the day, we were still 100 percent dependent on God for Aldo's healing. After all our failed efforts, I learned to never build my hope on anything other than God, and His perfect plan. We must allow God to do with our lives and our circumstances, as He pleases. The outcome will always be godly character in us and more glory for Him.

From the beginning, the Holy Spirit gave me promises to hold on to. Not in words I could hear with my natural ears, but through the Bible He spoke clearly to my spirit. To me, these promises are more real than a contract signed in court — because they come from God, and He is not a man that He should lie. These promises are my lifeline – and on the lifeline it is written: *God fulfills His promises; and He will never leave us, nor forsake us.*

With each new step on the water I drew closer and closer to Jesus, just as Peter did on the sea of Galilee, until I was so close I could hear His voice above the sound of the storm: 'Retha, you need to believe that I AM who I say I AM.'

The reason why people don't trust Jesus is because they don't understand the sovereignty of God, and they don't understand His character. Jesus said the only One who is worthy to be called good is God (see Matthew 19:17). No one else is worthy of this title. Because this is true, I definitely want to entrust my entire life to Him. It is the safest place to be!

People's negative words and unbelief distract us from God's promises and His faithfulness. I honestly don't get bothered about worldly opinions anymore. I choose to listen only to the truth of God's Word. Jesus' opinion is the only opinion that counts. We will get badly hurt if we put our trust in men. When we do get hurt, or slip and fall, we can always run back to Him. He will not show us away. He is faithful, even when we are not.

'He who did not spare His own Son,
but delivered Him up for us all,
how shall He not with Him also feely give us all things?'
- Romans 8:32 -

There are so many heroes of the faith to choose from in the Bible. Some of you may look up to Joseph, or Moses, or Abraham, because you can identify in some way with them. I choose a woman whose name isn't even mentioned — the woman suffering from the issue of blood in Mark 5.

Unlike most of the other heroes, her legacy is only a few sentences in the Bible. But it captivates my heart! As with her, Jesus is my last hope. There were many years of my life that I spent only looking at Jesus from a distance, just as she did when she stood at the edge of the crowd. The Man of God seemed so far away. But in a moment of desperation, she resolved to get close to Him, even if it meant getting trampled in the process. Her mind was made up. She *would* get close enough to touch Him, and nothing and no one would be able to stop her.

She pushed her way through the crowd until she came within a few feet of Him, but she still wasn't close enough. As a last resort, she laid down on the ground flat on her face, desperately seeking, stretching...stretching...stretching – until she finally touched the hem of His cloak. That was all she needed.

One touch and she was healed.

Jesus didn't have to say a word. The healing nature of God was just waiting for a touch of faith to be released. Listen closely. This is the key. I can hear her thoughts in that day, as clearly as if they were my own: *'If only I can touch Him, I will be healed.'*

Tell me, have *you* touched Him yet? Because your entire life will be a testimony of that divine moment with your Savior. The moment you touch Him, your destiny will change!

While you are still pressing your way through the crowd, or stretching towards Him, you are on the way to your miracle. Don't stop short or give up, persevere until the end. Through *faith* and *patience*, we will obtain our promises! (see Hebrews 6:12)

This Jesus of ours is moved by faith, not circumstance. The moment you touch Him, nothing and no one will be able to separate you from Him again, because He has imparted Himself to you.

Jesus will heal me.
I will go and do what Jesus asks of me.
The two of us will go together.
Will you please keep on believing without
becoming discouraged? Go and work without being afraid.

Jesus sal my self
genees soos die genesing
van die vrou wat aan
sy kleed gevat het,
Haar geloof het haar gered.

> *Jesus will heal me Himself, just as He healed*
> *the woman that touched His cloak. Her faith saved her.*

Some people are not *one* with Jesus because it costs a price that they are not willing to pay. Others want to reason out how God works before they are willing to believe. When people want to pull me into arguments about the supernatural things of the Spirit, I'd rather walk away.

I believe the reason why people fight and resist the supernatural (signs, miracles, and wonders) is because they haven't touched Him yet. Jesus warns us: *'Take heed what you hear. With the same measure you use, it will be measured to you; and to you who hear, more will be given. For whoever has, to him more will be given; but whoever does not have, even what he has will be taken away from him'* (Mark 4:24-25). I don't want to give unbelief the opportunity to take root in my heart; I want my heart to be established by truth.

> 'But the natural man does not receive
> the things of the Spirit of God, for they are foolishness to him;
> nor can he know them, because they are spiritually discerned.'
> *- 1 Corinthians 2:14 -*

> *My only hope is that Jesus heals me more and more every*
> *day. Mommy, the angels and I were with Jesus again.*

In the Gospel of Mark, Jesus says: 'If you can only believe, all things are possible!' (see Mark 9:23) Why? Because you *know* Him who makes all things possible.

After walking a very narrow road of faith for the past five years, here is what *faith* is to me: Jesus Christ *in* me, manifest through the fulfillment of the Word of God. Simply put: faith is when we believe Jesus is who He says He is. So many times the Lord has said to my heart, 'Only when you see the invisible, can you do the impossible! You need to look through My eyes, Retha.' I think the Lord has to remind me so many times, because my circumstances make it easy to forget. His Word stays true, no matter how difficult life might be.

In Hebrews 11:1 we find the Bible's definition of faith: *'Now faith is the assurance (the confirmation, the **title deed**) of the things [we] hope for, being the proof of things [we] do not see and the conviction of their reality [faith perceiving as real fact what is not revealed to the senses]'* (AMP).

Most people look at Aldo and only see a broken body. They may even feel sorry for him. When you look through the flesh, you will only see a young boy who speaks slowly, walks with difficulty, full of cuts and bumps on his face, and a hanging left eye.

Let me tell you what I see: I see a man of God, still in the hands of the Potter. I see a lion panting to get out of his cage to destroy the works of the enemy. I see a boy who loves Jesus with all his heart and trusts Him with his life. I see a man of faith!

I see that his flesh is not the determining factor of what God wants to do with his life. In fact, God doesn't see what we see. God wants to use us just the way we are.

At the end of the day, it is not even about Aldo's perfect healing. This young boy's future is predestined by a sovereign God. With all my heart I believe God has an amazing future in store for him. He is going to marry a wonderful girl, who loves Jesus just as much as he does. Together, they will travel across the world and testify of the Savior's amazing love, and lead many souls to Christ. (That is if Jesus doesn't come to fetch us in the meantime!) This is my title deed.

We all need to search our hearts and see what is written on the title deed of our faith. Do you even have a title deed for the things you hope for? Or are you just hoping things will work out for the best? Make sure that you put your seeds of faith out. Without the seeds, there can be no harvest.

Wees samed se ma en Vertrou God.

> *Be like Samuel's mother and trust God.*

Faith is to *know*, that you *know*, that you *know*, that God is who He says He is.

Once you've touched Him, will you come to understand His character, His love, and His goodness. Faith is not something you can buy over the counter, and no one can give it to you as a present. The responsibility is yours to press in until you come within arm's length of the King. *You* need to press in and touch Him.

Maybe you think miracles are only for the blind to see or the lame to walk. Remember, miracles don't come in boxes. God can do anything! For some of you, being freed from depression or bondage is the miracle you have been waiting for all your life. I have amazing news for you: the Father not only sent His Son to heal a broken body, but also to heal a broken heart!

In the Jewish custom (according to the Law of Moses), if a woman suffered from a flow of blood, she was considered unclean. The rest of the community would shun her, because if she came too close, they would be considered unclean, too (see Leviticus 15:19-27). So, the woman in Mark 5 not only suffered from a terrible disease that caused her much pain and discomfort, but she also lived a very lonely life. The moment she touched Him, her life changed entirely. Jesus not only healed her physical pain, but He gave back what the enemy had stolen: friendship, love, joy!

Depression, loneliness, anxiety, fear, lust, and addictions are all devices the enemy uses to steal from the children of God. This was never God's intent. His thoughts and plans are for our welfare and peace, to give us a future and a hope (see Jeremiah 29:11). Remember, God alone is good! His character is good, through and through, and we can trust Him with our lives!

To see the supernatural works of the Holy Spirit in my everyday life, is part of my miracle. To experience God's love and grace, is part of my miracle. To be dead to the opinion of man, and alive to the promises of God, is part of my miracle. To see Aldo hurt because of people's rejection, but still encouraging him to forgive and love, is part of my miracle. To come from the broken, selfish, me-myself-and-I Retha, to where I am today — where I can call myself a son of God — is the greatest miracle of all!

> *I love You, Jesus. Thank You that you were here last night while I was sick. You held me tightly and showed me I am going to be healed. Please show my Mommy and Daddy, so they won't be scared when I get sick. You are definitely alive, and You want us to trust You with my healing. I will be like Moses and show what Your glory looks like.*
> *Mommy, trust Jesus with everything you have. You will see that I am going to study and preach God's Word!*

Every one of us can touch Jesus. All we need to do is to walk in the Spirit, and press in until we feel the fabric of His garment under our fingers. We dare not listen to the lies of the enemy. I refuse to become discouraged by what I see with my flesh-eyes, I focus only on Jesus. Our healing, freedom, and victory are so close! It is inside of us, for that is where God dwells through the Spirit: *'the Spirit of truth, whom the world cannot receive, because it neither sees Him nor knows Him; but you know Him, for He dwells with you and will be in you'* (John 14:17).

> *Jesus says we will stand amazed at the power that will flow out of us when we believe in Him. Will you please keep on believing that I will be healed, Mommy? As our faith grows, so will God give us more faith.*

The Bible says of the Father of faith, (Abraham): *'He did not waver at the promise of God through unbelief, but was strengthened in faith, giving glory to God, and being fully convinced that what He had promised He was also able to perform'* (Romans 4:20-21). Abraham understood God's character. He did not doubt that God is who He says He is – the great, almighty *I AM*.

ek gaan eendag ~~ete~~.
werk vir Jesus
en ons sal sien sod
het gedoen wat Hy
gese het. Weet god
sal klaarmaak wat hy
begin het.

I am going to work for Jesus one day,
and we will see God did just as He said He would.
Know that God will finish what He started.

Because Noah believed, he and his entire family were saved.
Because Abraham believed, he received the desire of his heart.
Because Joseph believed, his dreams came true.
Because Retha believed, she will receive the fulfillment of her promise.
Because God is faithful, Aldo is healed (through Jesus' wounds)!
Thank You, Jesus!

Weet mamma alles
sal wees soos jy glo.

> Do you know, Mommy,
> everything will be according to your faith.

Aldo, Retha, and Josh

Dancing in the Spirit!

Lief vir 4 Jesus en lief vir God
weet mamma ons is uit gekies
as Jesus se ambasadeer op aarde
om Sy boodskap te verkondig.
God sal my gesond maak. Sal
mamma asb. God kies bo my. God
se ons sal ons werk wag ek sal
wees soos God vir my gewys het.

Ek gaan oor die wereld
werk en God se woord
verkondig.
Weet mamma god se god is so
trots op mamma want mamma

bly vertrou op Hom. God gaan
weer aan jou verskyn en jou
Sy heerlikheid Wys. Wees verseker
wie eerste sal wees sal laaste
wees ek weet weet god wil jou
oor die wereld stuur en 'n wereld wye
bediening lê.

> *I love You, Jesus, and love You, God.*
> *Do you know that we are chosen to be*
> *Jesus' ambassadors here on earth?*
> *We are here to preach His message.*
> *God will heal me.*
> *Will you please choose God above me, Mommy?*
> *God says we will do our job, and I will be as God showed me.*
> *I will work all over the world and preach His message.*
> *Do you know, Mommy, God says He is proud of you*
> *because you trust Him? God is going to reveal*
> *Himself to you again and show you His glory.*
> *Know, those who are first will be last.*
> *I know God wants to send you around*
> *the world with this ministry.*

Although very painful, this road with Aldo is a blessing. Through it, God has taught me how to walk by faith and not by sight. Jesus and I have become one, and that is addictive. I can't image my life without Him; my life was so empty before! In every situation I look into His eyes and I know something beautiful will come out of the difficulty. He takes my hands into His, and slowly, step by step, our walk in the Spirit turns into a dance. Few words are spoken. Close to Him, there is security that the world cannot offer. We dance on the rhythm of our Father's heartbeat.

Jesus says, 'You can relax, Retha. Let Me lead you.' In my ear He whispers, 'I have waited so long for this, My love. Thank you for taking My hand and trusting Me to walk with Me in the Spirit.' As we dance, I experience a new level of intimacy with my King. I don't say much. I only listen. He teaches me how to pray, how to trust, how to love — how to live and move and find my being in the sound of a heavenly melody. That is the first key to dancing in the Spirit: the music.

Deep inside the spirit of every believer, there is a fountain of living water. When the storms of life hit, we need to dig deeper (past the muddy water of the soul that can so easily be contaminated by fear and unbelief), until we reach the pure, life-giving, water stored up in our spirit. There we will find the faith we so desperately need, because our spirit is one with God's Spirit. We will also find a song of praise for our King. Faith will be our anchor.

When Aldo was extremely sick in December 2008, God revealed to me this power hidden in our songs of praise. Tinus took the rest of the family to see a movie, and I stayed behind to look after Aldo. He was just lying on the couch all day, still very confused and talking incoherently to himself. The one operation after the other made him very weak and it felt as if my own strength was also at a low point. It was as if a dark cloud had settled over me. I knew I had to fight the flesh with the spirit, and that the heaviness would only be overcome with a spiritual weapon. But I had to make a choice; it wasn't going to happen by itself.

I went into the kitchen to make us some hot chocolate. On my way there I decided: 'Up to here and no further! This heaviness won't get the better of me. I will worship the Lord, no matter how low I feel!'

My flesh felt weak, but my spirit knew my song of praise held the key to the victory – because then we no longer focus on ourselves, but our faces are turned toward God. Even though I felt completely empty on the inside, I was determined to dig until I found the streams of living water.

At that moment, it felt as if I didn't even have enough strength for one word, but what I *felt* wasn't going to stop me. I had made a choice – and my soul wasn't going to hinder my spirit from worshiping the Lord.

Deliberately, I formed the words in my mind. Starting with a soft hum, I fixed my focus on Jesus. As Father God can't resist faith, so Holy Spirit can't resist worship; especially worship in the midst of difficult situations. The more I sang, the stronger I could feel His presence resting on me. Soon I was on my knees on the kitchen floor, with arms held high and tears streaming down my face, and proclaiming: 'Jesus I praise You! All is well, the King is in control!'

The dark cloud of heaviness was driven back by the

streams of light flowing from my worship. There on my kitchen floor, Holy Spirit softly whispered to me, 'Just keep on doing what you are doing now, Retha. Jesus is smiling down on you!'

I took Aldo his hot chocolate drink and he wrote:

> *Do you know I felt the holiness when you sang?*
> *Jesus shows me how the angels are singing with you.*

That letter is so special to me! Because I felt how God opened the heavens for me, and sent me new strength.

The moment we start worshiping, we take our eyes off the problem and fix them on the Solution. The problem doesn't go away, but our perspective changes and suddenly everything seems different. With new perspective we will see Him for who He is, *El Shaddai* – God Almighty!

In my situation with Aldo, nothing changed in the natural, but in the Spirit there was an enormous shift. When we worship, we start moving in the realm of the Spirit, because it takes faith to worship when things look dark. When we worship regardless of our situations, our pains, or the trials we are facing; our spirit draws closer and closer to Him.

Jesus also knows what it feels like when the dark clouds come rolling in. When Jesus suffered in the garden of Gethsemane before His crucifixion, He prayed and asked the Father to remove the bitter cup from Him, but only if this was the Father's will. Abba Father knew there was no other way but for Jesus to be the Lamb that was slain for the sins of the world. But, He didn't leave Him without sending help. This Scripture is very dear to my heart:

> "'Father, if it is Your will, take this cup away from Me; nevertheless not My will, but Yours be done." Then an angel appeared to Him from heaven, strengthening Him.'
> *- Luke 22:42-43 -*

There on my kitchen floor, face to the ground, the Father sent angels to bring me new strength. My *song* ushered them in. My *song* was to the beat of His heart. My *song* was the music to our dance.

When you look at a young couple in love, you will find they speak a language only the two of them understand. They have the freedom to share the deepest secrets of their hearts with one another. They communicate on a higher level. This is prayer: a secret love language.

I didn't always know how to pray. I had to receive some practical lessons from my young son before I understood. I remember walking into his bedroom late one night, to find him kneeling beside his bed.

'Aldo, what are you still doing awake? You know you have school tomorrow. You should have been asleep a long time ago!' I scolded.

'No, Mommy. I am waiting on God. I talked to Him, and now I am waiting for Him to talk back.'

People say God doesn't speak to them. I want to ask in response, have you ever waited on God to answer? Prayer is not a one-way conversation. God wants to share His heart with you, just as much as you want to share your heart with Him.

One morning while I was dropping Josh off at school, Katie (who was also in the car with us) said that she really struggles to hear God's voice. Before I had a chance to answer Josh said, 'Katie, if you can't hear God, you are too far away from Him. Go closer. So close, that you can read His lips.'

During His ministry on earth, Jesus taught by using parables. The multitudes heard the parables, but only the disciples learned the truth hidden inside each one. Just as the disciples had to sit at Jesus' feet, so we too have to go and sit at His feet to find the revealed truth.

> "'He who has ears to hear, let him hear!'"
>
> And the disciples came and said to Him,
> "Why do You speak to them in parables?"
> He answered and said to them,
> "Because it has been given to you to know
> the mysteries of the kingdom of heaven,
> but to them it has not been given.'"
> - *Matthew 13:9-11* -

Lewe mamma is
hie wat die wereld dink nie.
lewe is eenwees met God. Se
vir mense jy het jou lewe
verloor sodat jy Lewe kon vind.

> *Life, Mommy, is not what the world thinks it is.*
> *Life is to be one with God.*
> *Tell people you lost your life in order for you to find it.*

In those quiet moments of waiting on God, not saying much and longing for the sound of His voice, more of my prayers have been answered than when I prayed with a lot of words. As my relationship with God grew in love and maturity, I started hearing His voice in the details of my everyday life. When I see Aldo smiling, I hear: 'I am faithful.' When I see his wiggle-waggle walk, I hear: 'I fulfill My promises.'

Prayer is no longer only those times when I pull my tallit (prayer shawl) over my face and kneel in my bathroom. Prayer is every time I talk to God (anywhere, anyplace), and best of all – I can hear Him speaking to me too!

Today I know any relationship that doesn't have good communication is in serious danger. We must not take the privilege of prayer for granted. We need to persevere in prayer until we break through and hear His voice.

Something happens in the spirit realm when we bow down before the King. When I pray, I get down on my knees and without saying a word, Jesus hears my heart: 'My King, here I am. I humble myself before You and seek the privilege of Your sweet presence. I am Yours. On my knees I will wait for You to come.'

Prayer is also the place where we win our battles. Jesus said that those who humble themselves will be exalted (see Matthew 23:12). When we decide to let the Lord fight our battles, we lay down our own strength, and wait on His arm to save. There on our knees, the Lord will give us the authority to overcome; because He will teach us to fight with the weapon of love. And love never fails!

God is the *Dream-giver*, but He is also the *Dream-fulfiller*. While we are sitting on His lap, He will blow His life-giving breath into our broken dreams, and give us wisdom and vision for the future.

God se jy het joy
hele lewe neergelê
help my oso weet jy
my hulp is van God

God says you have laid down your entire life.
Please help me. Do you know all my help comes from God?

Prayer is an act of intimacy. It is when the Beloved takes you into the secret place and speaks kindly to your heart. There you will hear Him say: *'O my dove, in the clefts of the rock, in the secret places of the cliff, let me see your face, let me hear your voice; for your voice is sweet and your face is lovely'* (Song of Sol. 2:14).

The last key to dancing in the Spirit is being one with your Partner – to anticipate His movements and be in step with His rhythm. You will hear a soft voice saying, 'Turn to the left, or turn to the right.' Without fearing you will obey, because Jesus is the One leading, and you trust Him completely.
To be one with Jesus is to be *in* Him.

As we dance, the Beloved whispers in my ear: 'Retha, I want you to understand the power in communion. The blood you drink and the body you eat, seals the sign of the New Covenant upon your heart.'

'For My flesh is food indeed, and My blood is drink indeed.
He who eats My flesh and drinks My blood abides in Me,
and I in Him.'
- *John 6:55-56* -

In the natural, the wedding ring a woman wears tells a story. It tells the world that she has a husband waiting for her at home. It signifies that she is taken and that she already has a sweetheart. A ring on any other finger is meaningless, but a ring on the wedding finger speaks a thousand words: It signifies love, commitment and loyalty. It signifies the covenant made between husband and wife.

The blood of the Lamb and His broken body set as a seal upon our hearts signifies the same. It tells the spirit world we are spoken for. It says loud and clear: *Bride of Christ!*

> 'And as they were eating, Jesus took bread,
> blessed and broke it, and gave it to the disciples and said,
> "Take, eat; this is My body."
> Then He took the cup, and gave thanks,
> and gave it to them, saying, "Drink from it, all of you.
> For this is My blood of the new covenant,
> which is shed for many for the remission of sins.'"
> *- Matthew 26:26-28 -*

The seal of the New Covenant is our wedding ring in the spirit. When the enemy walks past us, he sees the seal. More importantly, he knows what the seal implies: Jesus of Nazareth has bought this person with His blood!

To dance in the Spirit is actually so easy. We just need to let the Bridegroom lead. It is not our job to lead, we must only trust and obey.

Our lives will change as we choose this life.

The power in my tongue

Jesus weet elke mens se
wense. Wag net soos Abraham
Jesus se wie sy wysheid
soek sal dit vind. Leer hoe
werk gees jy sal wees
wat sal hy jou leer, hoe
werk die gees van mense
wys word want jy gaan
God se krag in gees
in spreek. Jesus se sy
Woord is wat jy moet inspreek.
Jesus se jy sal soos
hy spreek en mense woar
eers dood was sal daar
lewe wees. God se jy moet
vir iemand wat jou seer
maak seën. Weet nie hoekom
hie maar ek sien jou word
soos Amie McP.herson

Jesus knows each person's desires.
We need to wait just like Abraham did.
Jesus says those who seek
after His wisdom will find it.
You must learn how the Spirit works
and you will become what He teaches.
He will teach you about the human spirit
and you must become wise, because you will speak the
power of God into a person's spirit.
Jesus says His Word is what you will speak.
Jesus says you will speak like He did, and where there
was once death, there will now be life.
God says you must bless the person who hurt you.
I don't know why, but I see you
becoming like Aimee McPherson.

I believe the words we speak flow from the storerooms within our heart. With our tongues, we paint the picture of what is going on in the secret places of our hearts, for all to see. When the fire of God resides in our hearts, our words will carry the passion of His flame in the tone of our voice.

'If you confess with your mouth the Lord Jesus
and believe in your heart that God has raised Him
from the dead, you will be saved.'
- Romans 10:9 -

There is such power contained in our words! If only I could make everyone understand the enormity of this truth. The choice is ours: life or death, words that build or words that break, words of faith or words of fear. Our future (here on earth, and into eternity) will reflect the word choices we are making today.

'Death and life are in the power of the tongue,
and those who love it will eat its fruit.'
- Proverbs 18:21 -

If our words reflect fear, unbelief, sickness, or defeat, we can expect to eat these bitter fruits. Let's decide to build up our spouse, our children, our boss or employees (any relationship) with words that bless instead of breaking them down with criticism. We will see how quickly these relationships change into something beautiful as we walk according to this simple truth.

Lees Gen 1
Waar daar lewe gespreek
word kom daar lewe.

> Read Genesis 1. Where life is spoken, life will come forth.

'A soft answer turns away wrath, but a harsh word stirs up anger.
The tongue of the wise uses knowledge rightly,
but the mouth of fools pours forth foolishness.'
- *Proverbs 15:1-2* -

We must be careful about what comes out of our mouths. If our words don't bring forth good fruit, we must immediately stop speaking them. We must not give fear a voice by confessing the 'what-if' scenarios of the future. We must rather go into our inner room, where we are safe in God's secret place, and talk to Him about it. He is the only One who knows the right answer, and who can give us peace in times of uncertainty. If we can't speak good words, we must rather keep quiet entirely.

I learned the hard way that not everyone feels the same way about Aldo's healing as I do. God warned me about people who brought spiritual bindings upon my son through the negative, doubtful words they spoke about his healing. God revealed this to me and said: 'Retha, you must break every word of death spoken over Aldo, and replace it with words of life from the Bible.'

Remember, good always overcomes evil. When people ask me about Aldo, my response will always be: 'All is well – God is in control!' And that is the truth!

> *Mommy, please believe me – God says He is*
> *going to heal me. Please know God cannot lie.*
> *Jesus says we must keep on speaking words of life.*

> 'Look also at ships: although they are so large
> and are driven by fierce winds, they are turned
> by a very small rudder wherever the pilot desires.
> Even so the tongue is a little member and boasts great things.
> See how great a forest a little fire kindles!'
> *- James 3:4-5 -*

Our words impact our future, and they can turn any situation around. In the ICU, I kept on speaking words of life into Aldo's spirit, regardless of how much noise the machines made to distract me.

The machines said, 'His heartbeat is only twenty-eight, Retha! He'll never make it!'

But Jesus said, 'Only believe. Nothing is impossible for God!'

I chose to believe Jesus.

Over and over I proclaimed: 'Aldo, you will have life and life in abundance!' Those words brought life to dry bones (see Ezekiel 37:3-6).

> 'It is the Spirit who gives life; the flesh profits nothing.
> The words that I speak to you are *spirit* and they are *life.*'
> *- John 6:63 -*

Jesus rebuked the wind and the storm with words of faith spoken in authority. When the elements obeyed His commands, the disciples marveled (Matthew 8:24-27). If the wind and the waves bow down to Jesus, so will everything else. It is up to us to believe and confess His words. God will do the rest. 'If you confess My Words, you declare that you trust Me. My Word as promise is your seed of faith.'

The Bible tells us that for every situation, every problem, every sickness, every 'impossibility,' God is the Solution. I love to speak this Scripture out loud: *'Bless the Lord, O my soul, and forget not all His benefits: who forgives all your iniquities, who heals all your diseases, who redeems your life from destruction, who crowns you with lovingkindness and tender mercies, who satisfies your mouth with good things, so that your youth is renewed like the eagle's'* (Psalm 103:2-5). When I declare this, the entire spiritual realm knows that I lack nothing – God is my provider!

Careless words are like weeds in a garden. If we leave them too long, they will ruin the beauty. Choose your words wisely and bridle your tongue. Either you rule over your words, or your words (and the implications thereof) will rule over you.

> 'Either make the tree good and its fruit good,
> or else make the tree bad and its fruit bad;
> for a tree is known by its fruit....
> For out of the abundance of the heart the mouth speaks.
> A good man out of the good treasure of his heart
> brings forth good things, and
> an evil man out of the evil treasure brings forth evil things.
> But I say to you that for every idle word men may speak,
> they will give account of it in the day of judgment.
> For by your words you will be justified,
> and by your words you will be condemned.'
> *- Matthew 12:33-37 -*

Many marriages end up in divorce because of sharp tongues, kindled by the fires of hell. When you have truly died to yourself, the Holy Spirit will be in control of your tongue. By adjusting the rudder, the ship (which is your marriage) will be sent into a completely new direction.

In 2008 Tinus and I went to Rwanda as part of the *Living Ball Ministries* outreach team. On the last day, as a special treat, we went to see the gorillas in the mist. On the way back from the jungle, our guide made a sudden stop when he saw a man lying in a ditch at the side of the road. All of us got out of the vehicle and ran towards him to help. He was unconscious and there was already blood coming from his ears. From past experience, I knew what this meant – he was badly hurt, close to death. I immediately started speaking life over him: 'In the name of Jesus, spirit of death – I break your power binding this man's body. He will have life and life in abundance!'

All of us prayed over him, and I kept on praying in my heavenly tongue until I felt the peace of God releasing us to go on with our journey. There was no immediate change in the man's condition, but I knew it wasn't up to me to heal him. That I leave completely to Jesus. All I had to do was be His hands and feet here on earth, because God is the healer. We got back into the off-road vehicle and made our way home. We left the man with the other vehicle that also stopped to help.

The next day while we were waiting at the airport to return to South Africa, one of the tourists from the other car that stayed behind at the accident scene, walked up to Tinus wide-eyed. 'Sir, you weren't even around the second bend, when the man opened his eyes. We all got such a fright!'

Speak life and you will receive life. All we need to do is to trust Jesus; He is faithful and true. Life and death are in His hands. We just need to choose life.

> *Do you know, Mommy, God wants to give us back*
> *what has been stolen from us?*
> *Please believe me. You will receive your dream.*
> *Speak it and you will receive what you take in the Spirit.*
> *My job is to tell the world Jesus is alive.*
> *God says my life, my soul, and spirit are His.*

When I travel alone on my overseas trips, I take my Bible every day and speak Scripture into Tinus, Aldo, and Josh's spirits. Aldo always knows when I have been depositing Scripture into his spirit.

> *Jesus showed me how you were looking for Him all day*
> *long. He works while we are still sleeping.*
> *Ma'am, I can see myself preaching in front of hundreds*
> *of people. He says you trust Him with my life.*

> *Your angel is here again. He never leaves you.*
> *You have already trusted God with our ministry. God says*
> *He has the world ready for me to go and minister to.*
> *Did you speak to my spirit this morning?*
> *...Because I heard you.*
> *Will you please always speak life to my spirit?*
> *Do you know how much I love you?*
> *He gives us a spirit of love and not of fear.*
> *Mommy, God says you love Him very much.*
> *Please leave the lusts of the flesh.*
> *God says you must give your life only to Him.*
> *He will give you the desires of your heart.*

I gave a seminar on how it works to speak life into someone's spirit. There was a mother in the crowd who hadn't seen her son for the past three years. He ran off after he finished school, and she hadn't heard much of him since. She was desperate to see him again and make things right.

She grabbed hold of this principle with both hands and started speaking life into his spirit. 'My son, in the name of Jesus...' she would tell him how much she loved him, ask forgiveness for when she wronged him, and declare Scriptures into his spirit.

Not long after she diligently continued speaking light into a dark situation, he phoned her. 'Mom,' he said, 'I don't know why, but I can't stop thinking about you. I miss you and I want to come home.'

Maybe your spouse or even your children are not following Jesus. Take the Word of God and speak the Gospel of light into the darkness still in their hearts! Bind them to Jesus Christ in the Spirit.

'For it is the God who commanded light
to shine out of darkness,
who has shone in our hearts to give the light of
the knowledge of the glory of God in the face of Jesus Christ'
- 2 Corinthians 4:6 -

Take this Word and speak into their spirit. For example: 'Beloved, I now speak into your spirit the light of God that shone out of darkness to shine in your heart.' This light of the knowledge of the glory of God, in the face of Jesus Christ, has the power to drive out all darkness! The Word of God is the food our spirit lives by. Without food, our spirit cannot grow. I daily ask the Lord to make me and my family more hungry for the Bread of Life.

God says what is happening now is my head
needs time to heal. I know it will. You must just be patient. I
don't want to be like this. Jesus shows me what
it will be like when I am healed.
Did you speak to my spirit this morning?
...Because I can hear you, Mommy.
I know I react strange sometimes.
I don't want to be like this.
God knows I don't want to be like this.
God says all we need to do is to praise and worship Him.
From the bottom of my heart I ask you –
please don't lose hope.
His Word will not return to Him empty.
God knows you and Daddy are struggling,
and He wants to help you. I will be healed.
God says He doesn't want our works; He wants our lives.
My head will be healed, Mommy. Just be patient.
We will be happy when we minister together.

On one of my trips to Asia, a little boy came running to the front during a healing crusade, his face white, and a broken bone piercing through the flesh of his arm. I got such a fright when I saw him, and my first reaction was to want to call a doctor. If this scenario played out in my country, where hospitals and medical care are state of the art, he would have immediately been whisked off in an ambulance. But in the area I was currently in, there were no such luxuries.

I shut my eyes and asked the Lord what to do. Softly the Holy Spirit replied, 'Retha, this is a healing crusade. There are no doctors. Speak to the bone, and command it to heal.' I don't know who was more surprised, me or the translator, when I gave him the instruction to tell the boy: 'In the name of Jesus, this broken bone shall be healed. This bone will return to the way God made it.'

I was so scared, I couldn't decide if I wanted my eyes open or shut. I then told the translator (with eyes still closed) to instruct the boy to lift up his arm. I am sure he was still in a lot of pain, but my focus was on Jesus, not on what my eyes could see. Slowly he lifted his arm, and right there God did a miracle and healed his arm!

People started singing and praising God, and I fell on my face before the King of wonders. God is a creative God, and miracles are a part of who He is. In the Western world, signs, miracles, and wonders have become a topic of debate rather than a matter of faith. The wisdom of man is trying to explain the power of God, and failing to do so.

Jesus said to Nicodemus: *'If I have told you earthly things and you do not believe, how will you believe if I tell you **heavenly things**?'* (John 3:12).

Our words (anchored in our faith) must reflect *heavenly things* in order to see *heavenly miracles*! Remember, thoughts become words and words become actions. If we thus think upon heavenly things, and confess these things in faith, we will see heaven and earth meet!

Jesus wys my waar jy
Lewe spreek word wonderwerke
begin bare vinnig om
lewe spreek.

> *Jesus shows me where life is spoken, miracles happen.*
> *Start speaking life soon!*

The sound of the last trumpet

Jesus, ek sal gesond word en wees soos U beplan het met my lewe. Sal mamma gaan en vir mense vertel Jesus leef. Jy sal sien dat ek sal self soos Sameul God se stem hoor. Wys sy een groot liefde soos wat Sameul hom geken het weet mamma dat Jesus my meeste kere in die nag kom sien. gewoonlik sal water gaan soos strome en dan staan Jesus daar. Want My praat dan mek my oor sy wederkoms wat baie naby is. Sy bruid is nie gereed nie. Sal eendag self gaan en die bruid wakker maak.

Jesus, I will be healed and become
what You planned for my life.
Mommy, will you go and tell people that Jesus is alive?
You will see that I will hear God's voice myself,
just as Samuel heard it.
He shows me His one great love, like Samuel knew Him.
Mommy, do you know that Jesus comes
and visits me most of the time at night?
Usually I will see a big stream
of water and Jesus standing there,
and He would talk to me about His second coming,
which is very, very near.
His Bride is not ready yet.
One day I will go myself and wake up His Bride.

Yes, I was in church on Sundays in my life before the accident. But, the other days of the week my flesh reigned over my spirit. For most of my life, sin and self were the blindfold that kept me from beholding the glory of the Lord. I walked circles around the decision of truly laying down my life, and kept postponing it by justifying my actions. Before the accident I was lukewarm and that would not be acceptable to the King.

I am not saying everyone needs to encounter tragedy in order to meet the King. I am saying everyone needs to make a choice. My choice was made when I stood before the big red stop sign and bowed my knees. Only when I came to the end of myself, could I start a new life. To follow Jesus was now the only way forward.

You will be God's Bride like I am.
God will teach His Bride what she must say,
and He will prepare her for Himself.
Reveal His will to the West, the South, the North,
and the East to all the people.
His will is for His Bride to be ready when He comes.

> *You must tell His Bride she must make*
> *the decision herself to lay down her life.*

Early one morning Aldo started blowing the shofar (ram's horn) loudly into each of the four wind directions. He stood at the different corners of our house and blew to the North, the East, the South, and the West.

'Aldo, what are doing? You are going to wake up the neighbors!' I argued with him.

'Mommy, Jesus said I must wake up His Bride. Her spiritual ears will hear the call.'

That morning God revealed something new to me about His Bride: 'Retha, Jesus is on His way for His Bride – she will be a Spirit-Bride. She walks and lives in the Spirit and her spirit-senses are alert. Jesus will easily recognize her; she is totally set apart from the world.'

It is useless to prepare a Spirit-Bride through the flesh for her Bridegroom. I often see books with the ten-steps to be prepared for the big day. First of all, if the Bride is not walking in the Spirit, she won't be ready. That is the reason Holy Spirit often warns me: 'Retha, My Bride needs to fine-tune her spirit ears; the sound of the last trumpet will be heard in the Spirit.'

The Bride needs to live in the fire of God '24/7.' This fire of the Holy Spirit will cleanse and purify her in preparation for the King's coming. The fire of the Holy Spirit is also the wall that sin cannot break through. When there is no holy fire in our hearts, we must be careful; because sin can then creep in. The fire of the Holy Spirit is like a bright light inside of us. This fire will burn away anything that is not from God, and it will also purify our motives.

> 'Even the darkness hides nothing from You,
> but the night shines as the day;
> the darkness and the light are both alike to You.'
> *- Psalm 139:12 AMP -*

God is not intimidated by darkness. All He needs is access to our hearts, and that is a decision each person needs to make for himself. God will not break the door down, He only comes when invited.

When God created us, He gave us a conscience, and He gave us freedom of choice. Our conscience works like a blueprint of God in our hearts, so that we will know what is right and wrong. Remember, we were created in God's image. Unfortunately, worldly standards have placed a big question mark on the black and white of right and wrong, resulting in a confusing grey area. When we refuse to listen to truth, or justify our sin, we sear our conscience and sooner or later there will be nothing left convicting us of God's standard. To live in the grey area is very dangerous. It means we are lukewarm. And God says the lukewarm will be spewed out (Revelation 3:16).

When we surrender our lives to God, and give permission to His Holy Spirit to bring His light into every room of our hearts, we will be purified and prepared for the coming King. Purification is not always easy, but desperately necessarily. There is a holy Bridegroom on His way, and only a holy Bride can go with Him. The fire of the Holy Spirit is our preparation – it will make our hearts glisten brightly, as pure gold fit for a King.

I can hear Holy Spirit inside me saying: 'Retha, just as Hegai showed Esther how to prepare for the King, so I will prepare you for your heavenly Bridegroom. Being a spotless, unwrinkled Bride will be the end result if you choose to accept My instruction. Listen carefully to My guidance, as I understand the heart of Jesus better than anyone else. He and I are one.

'If you obey Me, you will be ready when the time comes. Obedience is the key to purification. When you are truly surrendered to Me, you won't find it difficult to be obedient and to serve. Serve others without expecting anything in return. That is to follow in Jesus' footsteps.

'This road of purification will undoubtedly hold trials and tests, but know that I am with you to face and overcome each obstacle. A lot of people want to experience the resurrection power of Jesus, but they are not willing to die to themselves. You cannot be purified unless your heart is brought through the fire of My flame, and it won't always be easy. But those who endure to the end will win the victor's crown of life.

'Always remember; *"I have called you by your name; you are Mine. When you pass through the waters, I will be with you, and through the rivers, they will not overwhelm you. When you walk through the fire, you will not be burned...nor will the flame kindle upon you"* (Isaiah 43:1-2 AMP). You are precious in My sight and I love you. Fear not, I am with you always.

'The hotter the fire becomes, the brighter the gold shines. Don't resist My flame. My flame will bring holiness, and it will reveal Christ in you – your hope of glory. Come so close till you experience My blue fire. It is the hottest part of the flame and it leads to a new level of purification. Not many push in until they experience this blue fire, and secondhand revelation is good enough for them. But I want to teach you the sound of My heartbeat – this you will only hear if you come very, very close.

'Many people know Me as a Companion, but not as their First Love. The blue fire is especially there for the Bride of Christ. There you will find intimacy and not a lot of words; some tears, some laughter, and an abundance of peace. Not everyone finds this place, because you only find it if you persistently seek.'

'Retha, what we have together is a treasure the world doesn't understand. If they only knew what they missed! The world is desperate for this peace and fulfillment that you have in Me, but they go seeking for it in all the wrong places. This secret shalom-place is only there for the Bride of Christ.

'I also intended intimacy for your marriages on earth, but only a handful of My children experience this gift – the blue flame of intimacy with their spouse. The biggest reason for this is that people think intimacy comes from works, and that it only takes five minutes to achieve. No, beautiful Bride – intimacy is passion, not action.

'Passion is when you come into My presence with praise, empty hands, everything laid down, and trusting Me completely. When you come into My presence take off all your masks, because with Me you can be yourself and share your heart without any pretenses. It is a place of intimacy, where you give yourself to Me completely. There you are washed with the blood of the Lamb, filled with Holy Spirit, cloaked with a cloak of humility, and I put a crown of joy on your head. The fragrance of holiness hangs over you, and I absolutely love it! I give you My hand and we dance. I enjoy the sound of your laughter and I help you when you give a misssstep, because you were so used to leading in the past.

'Now that you have given over to Me, I lead you. I answer all your questions and sometimes you only hear: "Trust Me" and nothing else. I can see how you enjoy every second in My arms and I see how your cheeks are wet from your tears of joy. With Me, there is no rejection. You don't have to feel ashamed to cry before Me. I will dry your tears. Your head stays on My chest for a long time as You listen to the sound of My heart, and learn the melody of your life. I let you listen to My heartbeat as long as you want, because it is important for you to remember what you look like through My eyes when you are faced with worldly opinions.

'I give you a treasure while you are lying on My breast – your promise. With eyes glistening you then look to see what I placed in your hands, and your knuckles turn white as you hold on to your one-of-a-kind treasure. No one understands why you keep on believing and trusting Me unconditionally; even when the circumstances you face scream out that you should give up. The reason is no one can see the treasure in your hands, and that is why you seem strange. The secret place is full of treasures for the Bride. My promises are your treasures – a word of knowledge, supernatural wisdom, visions, dreams, or sometimes just a simple yes or no for a question in your heart. It will always be firsthand revelation.

'Once you have heard the melody of My heartbeat, you will be able to dance in the storms of life. Everywhere you dance you will tell of My promise, of faith, of hope, and of pure love. The heartbeat of the Bride is a mirror image of the heartbeat of the Bridegroom: one crystal-clear sound of Love! says the Spirit to the Bride.'

He wants to show you His will for your life.
Stay in the Word. That way, you will know His will.

Mommy, God shows me His love for people is huge.
We must live only for God. Who will give his life to God?
Mommy, you show me what God
wants His Bride to look like.
How will I ever thank you that you never gave up on Jesus?

Purification is a process. Just like Esther had to go through months of preparation before being presented to the king, so the Bride of Christ, also has to go through a process of purification for the King of kings (see Esther 2:12). The end result will be determined by our willingness to obey. As with any journey, the first step is the most important. That step is the step of faith.

'And all of us, as with unveiled face,
[because we] continued to behold [in the word of God]
as in a mirror the glory of the Lord,
are constantly being transfigured into His very own image
in ever increasing splendor and from one degree of glory to
another, [for this comes] from the Lord, Who is the Spirit.'
- 2 Corinthians 3:18 (AMP) -

As we continue to look into the mirror with an unveiled face, we will be transformed into His image. No longer will it be necessary to try and please God with our works, but our works will be a testimony of our love for Him. We will be as a tree planted by streams of living water: always yielding good fruit (see Jeremiah 17:8). The steams of living water in us will bubble up, and we will give it freely to anyone who is thirsty, because we have in abundance!

Listen to Jesus' voice and please work for Jesus.
Mommy, please offer me to Jesus and never take me back.
Be holy, because His Bride is holy. Mommy, just as God lives
in heaven, so we will live with Him. Do you know, Mommy,
where God dwells sin cannot stand? His name is holy.

One night, Holy Spirit talked to me again about the Bride and how Jesus yearns for His Bride to be holy and pure. The next day, Aldo wrote this letter:

> *Show my letters to people. Show them what God says.*
> *Who will be what God asks of us – holy to God?*
> *Do you know, Mommy, God says you have a lot of pain*
> *and that only He can heal you?*
> *Please listen to what God shows you. He frees you from all*
> *bindings and makes you free indeed. Mommy, please know*
> *God says what I must write.*

The message is clear: If you want to marry a holy Bridegroom, you need to be a holy Bride.

After the purification process, Esther did something none of the other *ladies in waiting* had thought about: She asked Haggai (who understood the king's heart), what to take with her when her time came to be brought before him. Esther didn't only want to receive from him; she wanted to give her best to him.

> 'Now when the turn came for Esther,
> the daughter of Abihail the uncle of Mordecai,
> who had taken her for his daughter,
> to go in to the king,
> she requested nothing but what Hegai
> the king's eunuch, the custodian of the women, advised.
> And Esther obtained favor in the sight of all who saw her.
> *- Esther 2:15 -*

Esther thought about the king first and her own desires second. In the same way, Holy Spirit knows exactly what brings a smile to Jesus' heart. We will find great favor in the eyes of the King, if we set aside our own desires and only seek to please Him. (In the same way, God wants us to place our spouses above ourselves in our marriages. We each must give ourselves to our spouse, through intimacy, not works.)

The *Keeper of the women* (Holy Spirit) will show the Bride what she needs to take with her, and what she needs to leave behind on this purification road. Maybe Holy Spirit will lead you to start cleansing your house from objects that don't glorify God, or maybe He will show you certain things in your life (like your hobby, or body, or your children's achievements) that have become more important than spending time with Jesus. He may even lead you to distance yourself from certain friends who don't build your relationship with Jesus, but only break it down. Whatever it might be, Holy Spirit will reveal it to you, if your heart is open to receive.

Jy sou so Lyk omsy wil
te doen lyk plein wtg my
play station sy wil
vir my is heiligheid

> *You will want to look plain to do His will.*
> *Throw away my Playstation.*
> *His will for me is holiness.*

We bought Aldo a Playstation video game hoping it would help with His concentration, but he doesn't want to have anything to do with it. To him, his time is more valuable than wasting it in front of the television.

When Holy Spirit pinpoints something in your life, be sure to obey. Remember, the reward of Esther's obedience was favor with the King. Nothing you give up will ever come close to the reward of Him smiling over you.

Each one of us walks a different road, and what we lay down on the altar will be different for each individual. Talk to God about the things in your life. Don't do anything because I say so, do it because Holy Spirit leads you to do it.

> *Jesus says the work that I must do for Him is the reason*

The holiness of God will affect every area of your life: what you say, where you go, what you think, and even what you wear. 'Holy, holy, holy is the Lord God Almighty!' should flow like a stream of living water from your spirit.

Wees asb wat God van
jou verwag Heilig ek
weet jy sal gaan waar
God jou stuur weet jy
mamma dat God jou
sal wys wat om te skryf
in die nuwe boek.
Wie sal gaan en wees wat
God vra ek sal Jesus

Once Holy Spirit has lit the fire in your heart, you (as the Bride of Christ) have the responsibility to keep the fire blazing brightly. You need to make sure that you constantly add new coals to the fire so it won't burn out.

Nothing is more important in my life than to be one with Jesus. Because He lives, I can face tomorrow. He is the air I breathe, and with every new breath I want to glorify Him more and more. Jesus is coming back for a Spirit-Bride with a pure heart. She is a holy Bride, spotless, and eagerly anticipating His coming. There is only one true King. No one can compete with the love He has to offer, and His love is like a magnet that draws us into the throne room of God.

Today I know we will never be able experience true love in the world if we haven't experienced true love in the arms of Jesus first. That is why so many marriages crumble. The love we give to our spouse should be from the overflow of our love for Jesus. This love will never break down, it only builds up.

Are we ready for the last trumpet to sound? Are we prepared for when Jesus comes on the clouds?

This day may seem far away, like a little girl playing she is a princess and waiting for her Prince on a white horse, but we must be ready and prepared because that day will surely dawn – quicker than we think.

In the twinkling of an eye the trumpet will sound, announcing the arrival of the King.

> 'For the Lord Himself will descend from heaven with a shout, with the voice of an archangel, and with the trumpet of God.
> And the dead in Christ will rise first.
> Then we who are alive and remain shall be caught up together with them in the clouds to meet the Lord in the air.
> And thus we shall always be with the Lord.'
> - *1 Thessalonians 4:16-17* -

Jy sal mense leer
van god se koningkryk
en sy wonderlike liefde.

Wees Heilig vir Jesus
mamma sal vir mense
leer van sy liefde.

You will teach people about
God's Kingdom and His amazing love.
Be holy for Jesus, Mommy.
You will teach people about His love.

Are you ready to meet the King?

Lewens ver ander waarom god
wil hê dat jy mense moet
waarsku dat Hy oppad is
wees gereed as Hy ons
kom haal. Daar is 'n
bruilofsees wat wag vir almal
wie gereed is. Lees math 25

Lief vir u Jesus en dankie
dat u vir my gesterf het!
Lief vir u gees van god
gooi alles in jou huis uit
wat nie van god is nie.
Weet mamma dat jy geroep
is vir god self en dat
jy het vir Hom moet leef
Wie sal gaan en Sy woord
verkondig god sal my
gesond maak en ek sal Hom
dien solank ek lewe.

> *The reason God wants us to warn the people is because He is on His way. Be ready when He comes to fetch us.*
> *There is a marriage feast waiting for everyone who is ready.*
> *Read Matthew 25.*
> *I love You, Jesus, and thank You that You died for me.*
> *I love You Spirit of God.*
> *Throw out everything in your house that is not of God.*
> *Mommy, do you know that you are called for God?*
> *You must live only for Him. Who will go and preach His Word?*
> *God will heal me, and I will serve Him as long as I live.*

'Retha, My Word clearly says: *Those who seek Me, will find Me.* (See Deuternonomy 4:29.) *Teach My children to seek Me with their whole heart and soul. People don't realize they can draw as close to Me as they desire. I am seeking those who worship Me in spirit and truth.*'

Day after day I go to the throne of grace. Every time I leave the throne room I look different from when I entered. Every meeting with the King is unique and special. There are no programs, no agendas, no religiosity. I present myself before the King, and I give myself to Him completely.

In my quiet time, I lie on my face, and with my spirit I stretch out to God. My head is covered with my tallit (prayer shawl) and I am set apart for My King. As we spend time together, Holy Spirit reveals things to me that I need to repent of, and as I obey and choose to turn away from these things, I know the blood of Jesus washes me clean. With all of my being I desire the Lord. My spirit, soul, and flesh yearn for Him. As I offer praise to Him and focus entirely on Him, I can feel how He draws me in.

Through the eyes of my heart I behold His glory. I can see myself, standing in front of His throne, with arms lifted high, because I want to honor Him with all that is within me. Gently, His fingers touch mine and I can feel His power flowing through me. '*Your love my God, is better than life itself,*' I think to myself as I kneel before His throne.

This is how I draw closer and closer to my God every day – we share an intimate love relationship.

Why do we struggle so to give and receive love? We even struggle to describe love, because the world has corrupted the purity of love and made of it something that it is not. Love is not lust, and love is not cheap. Love is a pure and holy passion. The secret is to first find love at the foot of the cross – that is the starting point. Only once we have tasted pure love from the King (and know what it is to be sincerely loved), can we begin to love others the way God intended.

John (Jesus' beloved disciple) understood something of this love. His heart was completely sold out to Jesus. Because John understood love, God could entrust him with the most significant end-time prophecy, the book of Revelation. John, the beloved, was also the one who laid on Jesus' breast at the Last Supper. That is what love does – hearts start beating at the same rhythm and secrets are shared.

Time after time, as I lie with my head on His breast listening to His heartbeat, I can hear His voice like a perfect musical note:

'My desire is for you, My Bride. I want to be your First Love. I want to surround you with My love. I want to enjoy your presence and have you close to Me.

*'For such a long time My Bride has been slumbering. She has busied herself with other things, while forgetting that which is so important – intimacy with Me. The world outside has been corrupted, and even in most marriages people think the new love-language is **works**. No, there is only one love-language:*

> 'This is My commandment,
> that you love one another as I have loved you.
> Greater love has no one than this,
> than to lay down one's life for his friends.'
> *- John 15:12-13 -*

'My Bride must understand the hour she is in – there is no time to waste. Wake her up, her spirit must be ready. The Bridegroom is coming and the feast is prepared. She must

know and love and serve her Bridegroom. Not from a distance. Not merely with works. Not with head-knowledge, but heart-knowledge, in spirit and truth! Tell My Bride to choose the better portion that can never be taken away from her' (see Luke 10:42).

> *Jesus and I went up together, and the two of us were at the sea. I was with Him in heaven. I see life there, and there are a lot of people.*
> *Who was the angel that was here a while ago?*
> *He is always with you, and I know you can see him.*
> *God says I will be ministering very soon. God says what is going to happen now is you are going to go to New Zealand, and He is going to give you new fire.*
> *There is anger on the earth where the enemy dwells.*
> *People need to be reconciled to God –*
> *because Jesus is on His way. Please be ready. I saw Him.*
> *Please be ready, and tell the people!*

'I want My Bride to love Me with all her heart, soul, and strength. I desire to sit on the throne of first-love in her heart. When I made her, I designed that place especially for Myself. Everything I do starts in the secret places of the heart – because that is where I dwell.

'I have loved My Bride since the beginning of time. She must be set apart from the world – that is holiness unto God. The world will try and teach her that everything should be comfortable and easy, but I want to build her character. My plan for her is far greater than she can dream or imagine, but in order for her to walk in her destiny, she has to die to herself and her own agendas. That is why I desire for her to get to a place of complete dependency on Me, and not to rely on her own strength. My dream is for her to be My hands and feet in a broken world.

'Remember, when I walked on the earth I came to serve. My Bride will walk in My footsteps when she serves others, and not always expecting to be served.

'My Bride, do you want to wash My feet? Then wash the feet of your brothers and sisters. This is love – to serve others in humility, even those who don't deserve it. Always remember these words, they are so important:

> "'But I say to you, love your enemies,
> bless those who curse you, do good to those who hate you,
> and pray for those who spitefully use you and persecute you,
> that you may be sons of your Father in heaven;
> for He makes His sun rise on the evil and on the good,
> and sends rain on the just and the unjust.
> For if you love those who love you, what reward have you?...'"
> *- Matthew 5: 44-46 -*

> Jesus knows you want to please Him, and He is proud of you.
> You were on Mount Carmel last night and Jesus showed you,
> you have changed. Jesus says you must go to Israel
> because He wants to teach you.
> You must trust Him.
> He will give you the wisdom you need.
> Jesus is here with us.
> Don't become weary in your job.
> Work, because Jesus is on His way.

'No weapon is stronger than love, because I am love. When I come to fetch My Bride, I will recognize her by the cloak of humility around her and the streams of living water flowing from her heart.

'It breaks My heart when My Bride chooses to place other things above Me. I want to be her First-Love, and that is why I give this warning:

> "I know your works, that you are neither cold nor hot.
> I could wish you were cold or hot.
> So then, because you are lukewarm, and neither cold nor hot,
> I will vomit you out of My mouth.'
> *- Revelation 3:15-16 -*

'My Bride, test yourself with these words. When you speak about Me, is there a fire of love burning in your heart? If not, you are busy with tradition and not ready for My return. Today, is not too late, My Bride. Return to your First Love, for I am coming quickly.'

> **'But I have this against you,**
> **that you have forsaken your first love.'**
> *- See Revelation 2:4 -*

Dear Bride,

Jesus is calling you by your name and asking for your hand. See this letter as yet another invitation to His fast approaching wedding feast. Don't resist Him – lay everything down and listen to His constant knocking on the door of your heart.

It is His desire for an intimate love relationship with you. He wants you to be one with Him, and to worship Him in spirit and truth. The God of all creation planned this day for you to hear how much He loves you.

He is on His way; the time of His coming is very near. He is coming for a Spirit-Bride. Are you ready? Are you on fire for Jesus? Have you fully given yourself over to Him? Have you laid everything down? If not, now is the time.

Jesus is the only answer for a broken heart, a failing marriage, a difficult child. Maybe your life seems perfect, but deep down you know you are lukewarm and you realize you are missing something. Whatever it may be, believe me when I say there is only one answer: *Jesus!*

Yes, Jesus is alive! I experience Him in everything around me. I hear Him in Josh's bubbling laughter. I feel Him in one of Aldo's tight hugs. I smell Him in the flowers Tinus gives me on Shabbat. I experience Him in the cold wind against my cheeks. I feel His soft touch in the sun's rays on my hands. I hear His voice in Aldo's monotone: *'Mommy, I love you so much. Jesus is definitely alive!'*

Yes, Jesus is coming again – to fetch His beautiful, spotless, and set-apart Spirit-Bride.

Yes, Jesus will be here sooner than you think – look around you, the whole creation is screaming it out!

In exchange for your life, He gives you a life in abundance and eternal life with Him in heaven. He is not only looking for your heart, but your whole life – and especially the throne of first-love in your heart. Nothing less will do.

Jesus held nothing back. When He gave His life, He gave His everything.

Are you prepared to do the same?

Jesus, I love You with all my heart! Together with the Spirit and the rest of the Bride, I call out with all my strength: 'Come, Lord Jesus! Come!'

Epilogue:
Where Aldo is today

Het jy my enigste
hoop is Jesus. hy
wys weer hoe Jesus weer
kom op die wolke en
ons kom haal god se
dit gaan vinniger
wees as wat mense
dink. god se wie
hie hom u Jesus
werklik aanneem nie
sal verlore wees.
sal jy asb mense
se ek was in die
hemel en ek was in
die hel. hel is so
erg mamma asb neem
nou n besluit want
more kan werklik laat
wees.

> *Do you know my only hope is Jesus? He shows me how*
> *Jesus is coming on the clouds to take us with Him. God says*
> *it is going to be much quicker than we think. God says those*
> *who don't truly receive Jesus into their hearts will be lost.*

> *Please tell people I have seen hell.*
> *Hell is very bad, Mommy.*
> *Please, make your choice now –*
> *because tomorrow can be too late.*

It is April 2009 as the writing of this book draws to a close. Aldo has enrolled in a healing school for three weeks where they are mentored in the Word of God; especially in the area of divine healing. He enjoys every minute of it!

Although we sent him to *receive*, I stand speechless as Miss Patrys comes home every day with stories of how he *gave*.

He goes to those who are sickest amongst the sick and prays for them. He hands out the contents of his lunchbox to those who can't afford their own sandwiches, or he just puts out his hand to bless those he passes in the hall. This just shows me, that to serve others is already part of his being and a testimony that the King lives in his heart.

Aldo is looking forward to his graduation from high school and to start with full-time ministry. He already goes to poor communities in our area on Friday afternoons with Miss Patrys, where he prays for the children, plays with them, and gives them love in his simple way. People often ask me when he is going to start traveling with me when I minister. The time will come when God says *now*. Till then, I will wait patiently under His cloud of grace, because I don't want to run ahead of His plan. I will wait for God's perfect timing, because then the anointing will be there to protect us, as we walk step by step with Him.

In Aldo's life, I can see the freedom and the fullness of Christ. Aldo operates in a higher reality that functions beyond space and time, and is more real to him than what he sees with his natural eyes. He moves in the Kingdom of God and the unseen dimension. In Mark 4:11 Jesus explains it this way: *'To you it has been given to know the mystery* [secret or hidden truths] *of the kingdom of God; but to those who are outside, all things come in parables...'* This kingdom is built for life in the

Spirit and not for flesh and bone.

Aldo sows seeds of faith with his words every day. I believe that even if the enemy tries to cover these seeds with a ton of cement, God will still find a way for them to come up and yield good fruit. Everything must submit to the authority of God's Word, and that is why I will stand in faith until Jesus comes to fetch us. Hebrews 11:1 reassures me: *'Now faith is the substance* [realization] *of things hoped for, the evidence* [confidence] *of things not seen.'*

God acts on faith. That is why it is so important to keep on praying in faith and confessing His Word, and to persevere until the end, *'Without faith it is impossible to please Him, for he who comes to God must believe that He is, and that He is a rewarder of those who diligently seek Him'* (Hebrews 11:6).

Is Aldo's brain injury completely healed? No, not yet.

Is his speech perfect? No, not yet. He still speaks on a monotone and very slowly. Sometimes his words come out completely wrong, and this is the knee-halter why he can't minister yet. It is also the reason why his letters are so precious to him; when he writes, it comes from God's Spirit to his spirit.

Does he walk without stumbling? No, not yet. He still wiggle-waggles his way around, but we don't mind helping him. It teaches us to serve in even the simplest of things.

Does he love Jesus with all his heart? Definitely! He lives to love the King! When he falls on his face to worship, I can see that there is nothing more important to him.

> 'Looking unto Jesus,
> the author and finisher of our faith,
> who for the joy that was set before Him endured the cross,
> despising the shame,
> and has sat down at the right hand of the throne of God.'
> *- Hebrews 12:2 -*

I have set my gaze steadfast on the only One with whom nothing is impossible – the King who conquered sickness, sin, and death. The eternal King who gave His life for mine. This King will carry me through until the end, even if things don't happen exactly as I want them to happen or in my specific time. This King smiles over us when our broken lives bring Him glory. He rejoices when we surrender our lives completely to Him, and start walking in faith.

This King will complete what He started. He is the *Author* of this miraculous journey that I find myself walking in. I trust Him with my life, and I know He will sign His name at the fulfillment of His promises and the completion of His perfect plan, as the *Finisher*.

I am the woman who said: 'Jesus, I dare to believe Your promises, and take You at Your word!' And Jesus is the Savior who answered: 'Let it be according to your faith, Retha.'

You will recognize me as the one whose hands are holding on to God's promises with every ounce of her strength.

This is only the end of yet another chapter in our lives. As I stand peering into the future not knowing what to expect (because God is God, and He can do anything), I can tell you this much...

Because Jesus is alive, I can face tomorrow!

Retha

Author and public speaker Retha McPherson is also the founder of *Retha McPherson Ministries*. She travels extensively around the world as an ambassador of the Kingdom of God to proclaim the Gospel of Jesus Christ. The accident in 2004 set in motion a series of events that would change their lives forever. Retha scaled down on her professional occupation and started growing in ministry until 2008 when she went into full-time ministry. *Retha McPherson Ministries* is situated in Hartebeespoort, South Africa.

To contact the ministry, please visit our website:
www.rethamcpherson.com
or contact us at:
Tel: +27 (0)82 610 5757
E-mail: office@rethamcpherson.com
Postal Address:
Retha McPherson Ministries
PO Box 793
Hartebeespoort
0216
South Africa

We would love to hear from you!

Visit the McPhersons online!

- Stay updated with details surrounding the unfolding miracle by reading Retha's weekly messages and Aldo's latest letters.
- Order their testimonial DVD and/or Book (*A Message From God*, ISBN 978-0-620-38441-4) and other related products.
- Invite Retha to speak at your event.
- Partner with us to see lives changed and hearts won for the King of kings – Jesus of Nazareth.

www.rethamcpherson.com